Seven Keys
to
Happinesss

G.D Budhiraja

V&S PUBLISHERS

Published by:

F-2/16, Ansari Road, Daryaganj, New Delhi-110002
☎ 011-23240026, 011-23240027 • *Fax:* 011-23240028
Email: info@vspublishers.com • *Website:* www.vspublishers.com

Branch : Hyderabad
5-1-707/1, Brij Bhawan (Beside Central Bank of India Lane)
Bank Street, Koti, Hyderabad - 500 095
☎ 040-24737290
E-mail: vspublishershyd@gmail.com

Follow us on:

For any assistance sms **VSPUB** to **56161**

All books available at **www.vspublishers.com**

© **Copyright: V&S Publishers**
ISBN 978-93-505706-2-3
Edition 2013

The Copyright of this book, as well as all matter contained herein (including illustrations) rests with the Publishers. No person shall copy the name of the book, its title design, matter and illustrations in any form and in any language, totally or partially or in any distorted form. Anybody doing so shall face legal action and will be responsible for damages.

Printed at : Param Offseters, Okhla, New Delhi-110020

Publisher's Note

V&S Publishers have published a number of bestsellers on Personality Development and Self-Help category, such as 75 Ways to Happiness, The Success of Failure, Success 2020, Winners' Podium, etc. The present book, Seven Keys to Happiness is another milestone in this category. Here, the author has highlighted the seven salient steps or keys that are essential to attain Happiness, which is the ultimate aim of each and every soul on this Earth.

As you go through the book thoroughly, you will realise that basically 'Happiness is a State of Mind' that can be achieved only through contentment and peacefulness. If you are contented or satisfied with your life and your mind is at peace—Happiness will automatically follow. So, in order to lessen your anxieties, tensions, stress, fear, etc., and bring your mind to a peaceful state, one has to practice the Seven Keys or Steps discussed elaborately in the book. These are: Work with Passion and Zest, Live Life to the Fullest, Live in the Present, Live Free from Attachments, Maintain a Good Health, Be Contented, Love all and Cheer up and Think Positively and have Happy Thoughts.

Actually, the main purpose behind publishing such Self-Help or Personality Development Books are to motivate the people to work harder in their respective lives to achieve their desires and targeted goals and attain true Happiness, as all of us ultimately wish to be Happy, isn't it? If one's mind is possessed with stress, tensions, fear, jealousy and such other negative feelings, one cannot remain happy. Therefore all negativities, pessimistic approach towards life, etc., need to be completely abandoned in this pursuit for Happiness.

Hope the book serves its purpose well in helping you (our esteemed readers) to seek Happiness in your day-to-day lives, transforming your entire Personality!

Contents

Publisher's Note 3
Introduction 7

PART – 1
Causes of Unhappiness

Chapter – 1
What Constitutes Happiness.. 11
Chapter – 2
Causes of Unhappiness 18

PART – 1
Seven Steps to Happiness

Chapter – 3
Work with Passion and Zest – Live Life to the Fullest-
Be Decisive 30
Chapter – 4
Change is Constant – Live in the Present 39
Chapter – 5
Live Free from Attachments 48
Chapter – 6
Good Health – You Can Stall Ageing 54
Chapter – 7
Be Content which will Lead to Happiness 64
Chapter – 8
Love and Cheer up — be Content in Your Day-to-day Life ... 69
Chapter – 9
Always Think Positively and Have Happy Thoughts 78

Chapter – 10
Laughter / Humour is God's Gift for Happiness 88
Chapter – 11
The Various Steps to Happiness 101

PART – III
Thoughts To Happiness
Food for Thought 112

Introduction

To seek happiness is a sign of *health* and *sanity*. The founding fathers of the United States acknowledged this indirectly when, on July 4, 1776, they declared the "Pursuit of Happiness" to be one of the "unalienable Rights." Happiness has been called the American Dream. But it is the dream of all peoples and races, so long as their vital powers are not sapped. Only those who are enervated will choose unhappiness, pain, or suffering over joy and delight. I am not merely talking about pleasure or amusement when I mention happiness or joy. I mean bliss, ecstasy, rapture, felicity – what the sages of India call *Ananda*.

Could it be a sign of our times that so much attention, energy, time and money are invested in the contemplation of disaster, misfortune, crime, war, conflict, trouble and violence of one kind or another? We read about all kinds of adversities in the papers, see them on TV, hear about them on radio and gossip about them with our friends and co-workers. It seems that we are intent on bombarding each other with bad news. Somehow, it keeps the adrenaline going — and we do tend to confuse stress with aliveness.

Then, suddenly, for one reason or another, we come to a halt and ask ourselves: Am I happy? Am I happy living like this, doing what I am doing? The fact is, we would not be asking ourselves these questions if we were not experiencing unhappiness. We maybe blessed (or cursed, as the case maybe) with material plenty, and yet, we maybe deeply disturbed. Why? Most of the time, we do not know a cure for our distress. Sometimes, we imagine that if the right job turned up or the right man or woman came along, all would be well with us. Or perhaps, we feel that a glass of bourbon or a nice long holiday might fix it all. But we are only fooling ourselves. The glass will become empty, and our vacation will come to an end, as indeed will everything else. Sooner or later, the same feeling of unfulfilment or unhappiness will surface again.

There are many people who would claim that they are generally happy. Happy even when things around them seem to come apart at the seams? Or does their happiness depend upon external circumstances or internal conditions? Can they remain blissful when their son has just totalled their car, or when they learn from their accountant that they own back taxes?

It is natural enough for feelings of anger or frustration to come up under such circumstances. The question is whether we can feel beyond these negative emotions and continue to be a loving presence. If we can honestly say, "yes", then we are in a state that has traditionally been celebrated as a highly positive spiritual accomplishment; maybe not yet enlightenment or self-realisation, but reasonably close to it. In this book, I have tried to reveal the important seven secrets of Happiness. No deep philosophy will be found in the following pages. They are based on a common sense approach. I sincerely hope that people who are unhappy today will become happy after reading and acting on suggestions made in this book. That will be my real reward which will boost my own happiness.

G.D. Budhiraja

Part – I
CAUSES OF UNHAPPINESS

Chapter - 1

What Constitutes Happiness?

The word, 'happiness' can never be defined to everyone's satisfaction, even in functional terms, as long as people insist on using the word to mean different things at different times. For instance, we sometimes use it to refer to quite short periods of intense satisfaction (properly called ecstasy): Sometimes we use it to describe a prolonged period, free from major worries or discomforts; sometimes we apply it to experience properly joy, and so on. Some people would confine it to only one or two of such experiences, while others would extend it to cover the lot.

All these experiences, one immediately notices, are marked by the presence of agreeable feelings and the absence of disagreeable ones. So what it really comes to is, we have got to study the conditions in which agreeable feelings are generated and disagreeable ones prevented. When we have got this clear, we can settle the limits of the word, *happiness* in any way which is convenient.

The point we have reached so far, then, is that we can legitimately attack the problem of happiness by trying to draw up a full schedule of human needs and seeing how far they receive satisfaction; and that in so doing, we must not confine our attention to single individuals, but must constantly bear in mind their interrelation with the society they live in. To draw up such a schedule of human needs is a considerable task, for there is little previous work upon which we can call. We shall have to start at the beginning and spend several chapters, justifying our conclusions as we go along. But before we begin this, we should know what happiness is not.

The assertion that we can approach the subject of happiness by studying the conditions in which agreeable feelings are generated and disagreeable ones minimised does not imply that happiness is to be attained by satisfying as many needs as possible. There is a hierarchy among men's demands; some are absolute, others admit of alternatives, yet others can be wholly dispensed within certain circumstances. Happiness is not the answer to a sum in simple addition. Neither is it the answer to a multiplication sum. The task is not to meet the demands to the fullest extent. As we know from the old law of diminishing satisfactions, there comes a point in meeting any demand when it is no longer a wise use of energy to proceed any further; it is better to switch one's efforts to a different field. The delicate interplay of our various needs will become clear as we establish a picture of what they are.

A second source of error arises from the fact that when a man cannot obtain what he really wants, he will accept a substitute. Substitutes, however, are never equal to the real thing in the long run and much unhappiness can be traced to the unwitting use of substitute satisfactions. In the absence of butter, margarine provides a very real source of satisfaction: It does not follow that we shall be wise to devote our best efforts to increasing the supply of margarine. Since this may seem rather obvious, it is perhaps worth pointing out that we constantly make this mistake in our civilisation. In economic terms, we assume that the existence of a 'demand' is good reason for supplying what is demanded. We also assume the converse: that we need not supply what is not demanded.

I need hardly to add that the use of substitutes is not confined to the economic sphere: On the contrary, it is the use of substitutes in the emotional and intellectual spheres which is of chief interest in the present context. The childless woman who lavishes affection on a pet, the routine worker who pits his wits against the compiler of crossword puzzles, betray the flaws in our society, considered as a milieu for happiness.

Superficially, similar to the use of substitutes is the use of anaesthetics. When we cannot meet a demand, we may seek to numb it. Consider the case of the man who, being desperately unhappy because some fundamental need is being frustrated, takes to drink, to numb his misery. Looked at mechanically, his action is well chosen to raise his 'happiness-index'. Yet no one but a maniac would regard alcohol as a valid cure for his misery. Yet this is precisely the mistake we do make – in that we consider a demand for whisky or alcohol, an acceptable reason for satisfying it and make no attempt to uncover the frustrations which cause a certain part of it. Still more generally, we accept the whole demand for goods, and manufacture them, without asking to what extent the demand is a synthetic one.

Pseudo – Happiness

Something which obfuscates many attempts to handle the

subject of happiness in terms of needs is the existence of what we may call *pseudo-happinesses* and unhappinesses; or, more scientifically, *neurotic needs.*

The miser demands gold for his hoard, the Don Juan, a steady procession of women, the masochist, perpetual ill-treatment of humiliation. Can we say that these appetites are needs? Even if psycho-analysis had not exposed their artificial nature, we should still suspect them, since we notice that the miser's gold does not bring him happiness, and the Don Juan is not long soothed by his conquests. Though the victim of a pseudo need is unhappy when it is frustrated he is scarcely less unhappy when it is met. In such a case, the road to happiness does not lie in meeting the need but in getting rid of it – just as the treatment for the chronic thirst of diabetes insipidus is not a copious supply of water but injections of pituitrin aided by a low-salt, low-protein diet.

The moment we recognise the existence of such a thing as an invalid demand it dawns on us that a great range of supposed needs can be stripped off the human personality and thrown away, leaving-it maybe-quite a simple range of primary needs on which to build our thesis. This at once recalls to us the view so prevalent in eastern cultures that the road to happiness is to be found not in satisfying needs but in reducing them. Thus the opposing schools of hedonism(satisfaction of demands) and stoicism (reduction of demands) are combined in a new synthesis. In this way we can meet another, well founded objection to many previous attempts to handle the subject of happiness in terms of satisfaction of needs.

Nothing absolute about Happiness

There is nothing absolute about the concept of happiness: It has a relative import and cannot be considered in isolation. It varies from person to person and has much to do with faith and hope, courage and ideals to live by. By and large, fear, uncertainty, confusion and greed are the mainspring of much unhappiness. Time-tested philosophies of the past help us somewhat to come to terms with what looks like the greatest challenge of our time.

But what precisely is happiness? This intriguing question is as old as the hills. According to Aristotle, happiness is not something which could be felt or experienced at a given moment. It is, in essence, the quality of a whole life, the happy life being a good life.

Happy is the man who has all the good things in life and has no need left to be fulfilled, so goes the *Aristotelian conception.*

But what happens when greed overtakes the sense of need? The slender borderline between need and greed tends to get blurred as the acquisitive instinct takes over and becomes the prime mover of human conduct and eventually, a major source of misery. Plato, therefore, defined happiness in terms of harmony within the soul and equated it with the spiritual well-being of a truly virtuous man.

Immanuel Kant, however, decried the entire idea of happiness, regarding the pursuit of one's own happiness as a self-centred act, motivated by narrow considerations. Accordingly to Kant, we deserve happiness by the virtue of our deeds instead of just hankering after it. But we need not always be consciously happy.

According to J. Krisnamurti, happiness is a state of which one is unconscious. It is only later, when misery strikes, does one realise how happy one was. Much depends in the ultimate analysis, on one's perceptions and attitude to life. Two persons in similar circumstances are not equally happy or unhappy because they are not on the same wavelength and their expectations are different. Two points, therefore, clearly emerge: the less one expects from life, the greater are the chances of one's being happy and vice versa.

Secondly, one should know one's own mind. This is not easy, but it is essential. Swami Vivekananda echoed the Upanishadic truth when he said that the goal of man should be not to seek happiness or avoid misery but to go to the root of it all and master the situation which is responsible for their creations.

But such a mastery can hardly be possible without the right knowledge. It is due to ignorance that there is always a risk of getting carried away by things superficial and evanescent and missing the reality. What is purely external cannot have an eternal import and it is only the knowledge of the ultimate truth that can reveal the reality.

Basically, truth is of two kinds that which is perceived by the five ordinary senses, and that which is perceived by the supersensuous power of yoga. Yoga is union with the true self or God. In its secondary aspect, it is a mode of achieving that union. The spiritual processes for realising the self were built into a systematised discipline by Patanjali. He referred to the control of the thought-waves of the mind for attaining the highest consciousness as the main function of the yogic gnosis.

It is necessary to overcome the harmful thought-waves by raising waves which are good or benign. Thus, the feelings of anger, greed and delusion must be counteracted with the opposing feelings of love, generosity and honesty. When the harmful thought-waves have been subdued, the second stage of the discipline commences.

If the water of a lagoon is grimy, the bottom cannot be visible. Similarly, only when the mind is made tranquil, is it possible for the knowledge of the self to be revealed.

Happiness is an inside job

Do you resent doing what you are doing? It maybe your job, or you may have agreed to do something and are doing it, but part of you resents and resists it. Are you carrying unspoken resentment towards a person close to you? Do you realise that the energy you thus emanate is so harmful in its effects that you are in fact contaminating yourself as well as those around you? Have a good look inside. Is there even the slightest trace of resentment, unwillingness? If there is, observe it on both the mental and the emotional levels. What thoughts is your mind creating around this situation? Then look at the emotion, which is the body's reaction to those thoughts. Feel the emotion. Does it feel pleasant or unpleasant? Is lean energy that you would choose to have inside you? Do you have a choice?

Maybe you are being taken advantage of, maybe the activity you are engaged in is tedious, maybe someone close to you is dishonest, irritating, or unconscious, but all this is irrelevant. Whether your thoughts and emotions about this situation are justified or not, makes no difference. The fact is that you are resisting what is already there. You are making the moment into an enemy. You are creating unhappiness, conflict between the inner and the outer. Your unhappiness is polluting not only your own inner being and those around you but also the collective human psyche of which you are an inseparable part. The pollution of the planet is only an outward reflection of an inner psychic pollution: millions of unconscious individuals are not taking responsibilities for their inner space.

Either stop doing what you are doing, speak to the person concerned and expressfully what you feel, or drop the negativity that your mind has created around the situation and that serves no purpose whatsoever except to strengthen a false sense of self. Recognising its futility is important. Negativity is never the optimum way of dealing with any situation. In fact, in most cases, it keeps you stuck in it, blocking the real change. Anything that is done with negative energy will become contaminated by it and in time givinging rise to more unhappiness. Further, any negative inner state is contagious: Unhappiness spreads more easily than a disease. Through the law of resonance, it triggers and feeds latent negativity in others, unless they are immune-that is, highly conscious.

Are you polluting the world or cleaning up the mess? You are responsible for your inner space; nobody else is, just as you are responsible for the planet. As within, so without: It helps in clearing inner pollution, and then the outer pollution will also cease.

Ever wonder why so me of the most successful people still seem unhappy? According to us, they have it all: looks, fame and fortune. Whenever we strive for something and reach it, there's a duality of elation and dejection. It is over. We do what is to be done next and the quest starts all over again. Somehow, the end result usually seems to be more exciting on the way there than when it is reached. The remedy is having inner peace and all the rest falls into place and becomes the icing rather than the whole cake. When we are happy with whom we are, we can go anywhere and create that same atmosphere of warmth. If we run away, we can change locations but the same situations are carried with us. Stay put and flow with all the ideas and solutions. Then wherever you roam, you will have a house of contentment.

There are characteristics of ourselves and our loved ones that should be recognised in order to curtail inevitable problems. One such aspect is that of poor problem solving. A difficulty can only be resolved when you take responsibility for it. Another characteristic is rigidity, inflexibility in thinking and behaviour. The more clearly we see the reality of the world, the better we can deal with it. Many people stop filtering any information unless it conforms to their map of reality so their views of reality are sketchy, narrow, and misleading. Views should always have the capacity to change when new information is introduced.

Do you realise that happiness is truly an inside job? It frees the heart from hatred and the mind from worry. It is respect, and communication with yourself. Happiness is something you decide ahead of time, so deposit a lot of happiness in your Memory Bank and make constant withdrawals. Use these insights for self-empowerment and for renewed awareness.

We cannot become happy; we can only be happy

But let us assume that we are not so fortunate. What can we do to become happy? The short answer is: Nothing! In fact, the more actively we seek out happiness, the less likely we are to find it. This is because all forms of seeking pertain to the finite, egoic consciousness(our everyday identity), whereas true, permanent happiness is the unconditional Reality itself, which transcends the ego. So all we can hope for in our search for happiness are pleasurable experiences, and we already know that they do not last.

But when I say we can do nothing to become happy, this is only half the truth. It would be unfortunate if happiness were to elude us forever. Happily, it does not. It is accessible to us: We must simply be happy in every moment. I learnt this secret from one of my teachers, and I do not think I would ever have discovered it on my own. *It sounds so simple-even paradoxical. Yet it is really profound wisdom. We cannot become happy; we can only be happy.*

Most people have experienced moments of joy or delight at one time or another in their lives. That means we know what happiness feels like—it is what we experience when our whole body radiates with joyous energy and we feel like embracing everyone and everything. In those precious moments, we are in touch with something more real than our ordinary self or the world that our ordinary self experiences. Our ego is temporarily suspended, and our consciousness and energy are stepped up. We simply feel overwhelming happiness and bliss, which has the quality of love. We can always remember, with our whole body, those occasions of extraordinary joy.

Whenever we are fully present as the whole body, whenever we centre ourselves, we get in touch with the larger Reality in which we are immersed. And that larger Reality is neither depressed nor problematical. Then our energy starts to flow more freely, and we feel a deep sense of security. We intuit that our true identity is untouched by any conflict or pain.

To remember to be present as the body is a skill that can be learnt. To be presently happy rather than to seek to become happy is an open option for all of us – in every single moment. We can either lose ourselves in fear, anger, sorrow, lust, jealousy, pride, self-complacency, and all the other egoic states, or we can feel through to the great pool of bliss that lies beyond them.

Happiness is our birth right. But we must claim it.

Chapter - 2

Causes of Unhappiness

Living in this age of constant gratification, economics flux, and fragile egos, happiness is increasingly elusive. Yet it remains the holy grail we search all our lives.

Leading a split life has been one of the greatest problems down the ages and that's why humanity all over is sick today. We don't synthesise things as a whole and since we have overlooked the wholeness of life, we live at the minimum and ultimately become victims of sufferings.

We view the worldly and non-worldly things as separate entities and that's where we fail miserably. Meditation and love, loneliness and relationship, sex and silence cannot be viewed separately.

Down the ages man has suffered simply because the problem has not been understood correctly. Whether it is a monk or a family man, both suffer equal amounts of pain. The reason is because they remain half, and to be half is to be miserable. On the other hand, to be whole is to be healthy and perfect.

Osho explains that "To remain half is miserable because the other half can't be destroyed. After all, it is your other half. It is not something accidental that you can discard. It is like a mountain deciding that it will not have any valley around it but without valleys the existence of mountain is impossible. They are complementary to each other. If the mountain chooses to be without the valleys, there will no mountain either. Thus, the mountain of aloneness rise only in the valley of relationship."

Similarly, poison and nectar are not two things but two states of the same energy. When it flows, it becomes nectar but when it's frozen, it becomes poison. In the same manner, music with silence can only be noise. That's the reason one should accept the wholeness of life and not live it in half. And for that being aware is very important.

It is our basic nature to seek happiness. Do we get it? When we look around, we find ourselves surrounded by suffering. We feel uneasy; that we are perched on an island of some happiness, surrounded on all sides by deep and dark waters of unhappiness. Is happiness just a mirage? The fact is that there is neither undiluted happiness, nor unabated unhappiness. Life is both. However, the nature of pain is such that it appears that the unhappy phase of life is interminable long.

The mind reacts to external stimuli and this could sometimes bring us happiness or unhappiness. For enduring happiness, the internal war that rages within our minds should first cease. We should come to terms with external ground realities. As physical training keeps the body in good shape, so also mental training helps in keeping the mind tranquil and balanced in the face of adversity.

Worry, Anxiety and Fear

Why do we worry ?

Everyone tends to worry about their romantic lives, their jobs, money, health, friends, family, exams, weather, weight, security, among others. For some people, worrying about everything under the sun becomes almost a reflex action. It's like an addiction where you have to get your fix, whether there really is a problem or not. At times, when you have nothing to do, you worry, times when you have too much on your plate, you worry, and times when you know there's no reason to, worry you still worry. All this despite that voice in the head telling you how unreasonable these worries are!

Till of course, a time comes when you just forget that there's more to life than all those fine lines on the forehead that get deeper and deeper with every passing day. Worry usually occurs when we find ourselves faced with a likely outcome we feel is beyond the scope of our control an outcome, we think will be wholly damaging and detrimental to us. But how can we be so certain? Maybe some good comes out of it as well. So why despair and agonise over something that may actually turn out well, or if it does not now, it might be okay in the long term?

The human brain is equipped with an elaborate system designed to register the emotions of fear and worry. This system serves an important function it mobilizes us to respond to danger by setting in motion a complex sequence of biochemical and physiological events. The adaptive side of worry is that it allows us to anticipate danger and take preventative actions. So, a certain amount of worry can be healthy. However, excessive anxiety and worry can, like anger and hatred, have devastating effects on the mind and body, becoming the source of much emotional suffering and even physical illnesses.

The chain of the cause and effect is extremely subtle. The slightest, invisible variation in an event could well lead to dramatic consequences in the future. Therefore, it is almost impossible to predict what will happen in the long term, and whether it will be good or bad because we cannot know all the variables precisely. Neither do we know how the fortunes and misfortunes of other people may forward or reverse ours or for that matter, too, how our fortunes or misfortunes may affect those of others.

Are you a worrier?

You are a worrier if you always see a glass as half empty. Every little thing makes you worry. You get into worry mode when you have nothing to do. You invariably find something to worry about. Everyone tells you that you worry too much.

When you worry, usually what happens is that rationality gets thrown out of the window and thoughts get muddled up. Emotions eventually play a greater role than logic, so you should try to write down what is worrying you.

Worry creates so many problems

A man having stomach pain went to his doctor. The doctor asked if he was having trouble in his personal life or at his job. The man explained that he was worried about some incidents that had happened at work with his boss and his co-workers. Was there something the man could do to change what had happened? "No," responded the man. "But it continues to bother me." The doctor said, "there is nothing you can do about the past. Close the chapter and move on. You are upsetting yourself and your stomach over something you cannot change." The doctor prescribed some medicine, and advised him to forget the past to help expedite the cure of his stomach aches.

The next patient was a woman with migraine. She explained that she was afraid of making a wrong decision about her future. Sensing that this was causing her headaches, he told her, "If you make a decision that turns out all right, there is nothing to worry about. If you make a decision that turns out wrong, you still have the option to rectify matters. No decision is irreversible. Make a list of your options; make a counter plan for each option and then act. Analyse the situation, and then act. Then take each step as it comes."

People either worry about a past that they cannot change, or they worry about a future that has not yet happened. Many worry over problems they anticipate or fears that never materialise. Many of our stress related illnesses are due to problems that we face mentally, psychologically or emotionally. What is certain is that there are always going to be problems.

Murphy's Law says that if anything can go wrong, it will. There does not seem to be anyone who has not experienced problems in life. Every time we solve one problem, a new one springs up. After a while, we begin to wonder if there will be a time in life when we can be free of problems.

Nobody said that life was going to be easy or that everything was going to be perfect. The question is, how do we handle our problems? Do we face them as a challenge and try to solve them, or do we fret and worry about them?" We compound our problems by worry and fretting because this added stress can make us physically sick.

The pressures of life are so great that they affect us physically and mentally. We find that people undergo anxiety, fear, depression and phobias. Offices of psychiatrists, psychologists and therapists are filled with normal everyday people who cannot cope with life's struggles.

Fear

Fear is the most common negative emotion. It is universal. It drains away our physical and mental energy. Fear is a great stumbling block to progress. The origin, type and intensity of fear varies from person to person. Nervertheless, fear haunts us all. It is a great shame that despite our inherent divinity, we continue to be held hostage by the psychosis of fear.

Every morning the newspapers are full of stories on crime and terror. There are reports coming in from every corner of the world, so much so that fear sets in as soon as we see the postman slipping an envelope into the mailbox.

The question seems more relevant when we find that in actuality many of these cases are false alarms. Why do we enjoy creating false alarms? Why is the mind so ready to believe crimes have come knocking at our doors? Why do we so enjoy reading about such cases and dismiss with little interest the crucial line that it was a false alarm? Why do we enjoy writing about it? Why do we enjoy talking about it endlessly on the phone or with our neighbours? Not all the above acts are conscious acts. Many of them we do automatically.

Fear is not an abstraction. It exists always in relation

to something. That something could be apparent or in our subconscious mind. But its relational aspect cannot be ruled out. Fear can be of death, ailment, loss of reputation, failure in examination, a ghost, black magic, soul possession, or loss in trade. It could be anything.

Fear begets anxiety. Anxiety together with doubt and indecisiveness plays havoc with our physical and mental health. Fear hampers initiative, suppresses skills, strangles ingenuity. Fear harnesses mental weaknesses which results in constant stress and strain. It brings misery and misfortune.

Fear does not mean being foolhardy. Fearlessness means being aware and having knowledge. We fear that of which we know least or do not know at all. Half baked knowledge is the breeding ground of fear. When we have adequate knowledge, we have less fear.

There are two types of fears, says psychiatrist Ashit Sheth. "The first type of fear revolves around our basic biological needs, that is security, sex and procreation. The second type of fear is socially conditioned."

Basically, the flight and fight mechanism helps us to help ourselves. It is only when this mechanism in our brain is under or overactivated that behavioural problems begin to develop. While most of us experience fears that are episodic and do not interfere with our daily lives, some people develop fears that can disturb or even threaten their capacity to live normal lives.

Below I raise your some of the most secret bogeys.

Fear of losing job

Even in today's booming market, an increasing number of men and women are finding themselves shunted from their jobs. Either their job profile has become redundant or they are the victims of downsizing by the company. While most women tend to take it in their stride, men, in general, can't. A man's attachment to his job is programmed deeply into his emotional makeup.

Fear of failure

This fear stems from the fact that people are afraid they may not be able to perform according to expectations. This is very common today among young students. They set very high standards for themselves and then are afraid that they will not be able to achieve those standards. In most of these cases, they are good students. But this also happens with adults who are so afraid of performing in an imperfect manner that they refuse to perform altogether. Their fear of inadequacy makes them feel inadequate, when in fact, they maybe capable or even more than capable to handle the job. Suppose a girl has a flair of designing, but when her friends suggested that she take it up as a career, she said she couldn't. She protested that she wasn't good enough; she was so afraid of failure that she had given up before even attempting it.

Fear of aging and growing old

This is a problem that affects both sexes equally. And it's not just a question of a wrinkle or the first grey hair. It's more about growing old alone, ending up in a wheelchair and having no one to look after them.

Fear of death

People act as if death is contagious. Death is as natural as life. It is the part of the deal we made. It is natural to die. The fact that we make such a big hulla baloo over it is all because we do not see ourselves as part of nature. We think because we are human we are above Nature. We are not. *Everything that gets born, dies. Death ends life not relationship.*

Loss and grief

Loss is a part of every life. The death of a loved one is perhaps the most dreaded loss, but there are others: the loss of good health, the loss of a physical or mental capability, the loss of a job, the loss of a relationship, even the loss of a treasured possession. No loss is welcome, and all are painful. Still, people recover from loss, though for some the recovery is protracted and difficult. And with recovery comes the opportunity to learn and grow, to be wiser even if sadder.

Grief in case of bereavement

Although every bereaved individual experiences loss in a unique way, psychologists have identified responses that is typical and normal. More than simply being normal, this type of grieving leads to resolution and recovery.

Take the case of deceased relative. The first phase of mourning often begins with sensations of shock and numbness, even if the loss was predictable and slow in coming. It can take months to get over the shock. In initial stages, mourners are preoccupied with thoughts and memories of the deceased and may experience the sensation that the lost one is physically near, especially at night. Common, too, is an intense searching and yearning for the deceased.

The early stage of mourning are frequently coloured by feelings of guilt and anger ("What did I do?" or "I wish I had been there for him more often" or "Why did he/she do this to me?"). Bargaining is common ("If only I could..."), as is protest ("What did I do to deserve this?"). Pangs of grief are accompanied by periods of anxiety and restlessness, but bereaved individuals are usually able to function during the busy and stressful early days of making arrangements.

The second stage of grief is frequently characterised by disorganisations and depressions. This is the most painful phase as well as the most protracted, lasting three to six months in many cases. Instead of feeling close to the lost one, the mourner feels isolated and terribly alone.

Abnormal grief

Grief is a necessary process that leads to healing but if it goes away, it can lead to illness, either psychological or physical. Abnormal grieving can take many forms, ranging from denial of feelings to an unrealistic portrayal of the lost loved one as a perfect individual. Most often, though, the result is depression. It can be hard to determine when normal grief becomes pathological depression, but psychiatrists have proposed criteria for a diagnosis of Complicated Grief Disorder.

The loss of a spouse is more common for women, but it's more serious for men. Why do widowers face an increased risk of death? Doctors can only speculate about several possible explanations. The loss of a caregiver could be part of the answer but since the impact is substantially greater in healthy men than in ill men (who may depend on a spouse for care), that can't be the whole story. Most likely, intense grief adversely affects the body's stress hormones, nervous system, and immunologic apparatus; it's the same way-extreme way-in which fright and natural disasters can trigger sudden cardiac death in men.

Stress and depression

Like happiness, a certain amount of sadness is natural. When we lose a loved one or a job, or experience a big disappointment, it's normal to feel sad. At mid-life, it's normal to feel a little sad when the kids go off to college or leave home to begin families of their own, it is normal to feel tired a little sooner at work, normal to feel a twinge of regret every now and then when you think of dreams you had that may never be fulfilled.

But when that sadness doesn't go away...when fatigue colours your entire approach to life and saps your energy, when regret drains your enthusiasm, that's *depression.* And it is a problem you must do something about because depression can affect your life and health in many negative ways. If you're depressed, you won't be the same at work or at home. Your productivity can come down endangering your livelihood. Your family life can suffer. And in some circumstances, untreated depressions can lead you to abandon all hopes.

You do not need a medical diagnosis to know when your stress level is out of control. What's more, scientists are just beginning to uncover some surprising physical repercussions of unchecked depressions. Depressions weaken your immune system's ability to fight off disease. If you're depressed and you smile, it's a deadly mix. Not only are depressed smokers less likely to quit, they're also more likely to develop cancer. Depression heightens your heart disease risk, too! A Finnish study showed that all other risk factors being equal, depressed men had two to four times greater plaque build up in their arteries than men who were not depressed.

When you feel low and suffer bouts of depression, it affects you work and relationship. What is that which happens within you? Fundamentally, you expected something to happen and it did not happen. You expected somebody or something to be your way and it did not happen. In other words, you are simply against what's happening; that's all. Maybe you are against a person; maybe you are against a whole situation; maybe you are against life itself. Accordingly, the depression will run deeper and deeper.

Why are you against something? Only because things didn't go your way, isn't it? Why should the world go your way? Or you have no acceptance of the situation, and you have a hypersensitive ego; that's why you get depressed.

Depression makes you cynical; it is deeply self-damaging. Usually depressed people will not cause harm to others; they will only hurt themselves. A depressed person is always trying to cause damage to himself. Why will a person go on hurting himself? Generally, it is to get sympathy. For a depressed person, normal sympathy is not sufficient; somebody should bleed with him.

Depression is more than a passing blue mood, more than a twinge of sadness you feel on hearing an old love song. When you're depressed, your whole body can be depressed, not just your thoughts and moods. The effects of depression show up in the way you eat, the way you sleep, the way you work and even the way you play.

Perfectionism

You need only to hand on to your daunting standards of perfectionism, and you can be sure happy days will never come.

The perfectionist's drive for success and accomplishment may seem, on the surface, very similar to that of the healthy 'striver for excellence.' However, the underlying dynamics are very different. Strivers after perfectionism are idealistic – often to a pathological degree. Theirs is a negative motivation – to avoid disapproval, rejection or criticism – from other people, or just from the inner critic in their head. Because perfectionists will accept nothing less than, well, 'perfection', they are rarely satisfied with the outcome. In their own eyes, they never seem to do things well enough to warrant a feeling of satisfaction. They are so completely focussed on the destination that they never enjoy the journey.

Are you a perfectionist?

Perfectionists generally know themselves for what they are. But if you're just beginning to wonder, after reading the preceding paragraphs, whether you might be a perfectionist, you probably are, at least to some degree. If you want to make sure, check whether the following traits of the perfectionistic personality sound familiar.

Unrealistic standards

Just being 'almost perfect' is not enough for a perfectionist: it's tantamount to falling down on the job. The perfectionist is perennially assailed by the feeling that he/she should have done more, in less time, than is reasonably possible. All-or-nothing, black-and-white thinking is typical of the perfectionist: *if it's not perfect, it's a failure.*

A hypercritical perspective

The tiniest mistakes and imperfections are magnified by perfectionists into "just won't do" proportions. They home in and obsess over minor flaws – such as a word or a hair out of place

– and have trouble seeing that the job overall has not been well done. 'Finicky' and 'fussy' are words that justifiably describe them.

Not only are perfectionists highly critical of themselves but also of others. Rather than do an imperfect job themselves, they end up spending a good amount of time frowning upon the imperfections of others. Criticisms then become like a recording loop in their brain playing its jarring tune over and over: A mirror before he she leaves the house.

Chronic depression

Because their initial goals are set so high, perfectionists beat themselves up every time they go unmet. Unable to bounce back easily from disappointment, they wallow in depression. It takes them a very long time to climb out of that pit of misery and move on to the next challenge.

Their depressions can pretty much take on a life of its own: There are perfectionists who view their depressions as flaws and become more depressed.

Anger and stress

Perfectionists feel impotent if they haven't done their best (or surpassed it) and this can bring on a lot of anger, often hidden and controlled. On the other hand, their critical take on the imperfections of others can also bring on anger, in this case the self-rightiest kind.

It's hard work having to be on top all the time, so perfectionism unsurprisingly also trails in a load of stress.

Resentment and self-pity

The lack of real achievement is a common outcome with perfectionists. They lose so much time and energy on small irrelevant details of projects, tasks, even mundane daily activities, have organisational rituals which seem pointless to others, always seem to be needing so much more preparation before getting started on something, that they end up actually achieving far less than others who get on more briskly with the imperfect present.

Faced with the fact that they are notching up fewer achievements than others, perfectionists build up a chache of negative emotions: Resentment and Jealousy – *Why should others get more rewards than I do when their performance is so average, so full of holes I could pick, when I have a far greater potential for perfection than they do?* Self-pity – *Poor me; why can't people see beyond my immobilisation to my true, never-expressed talents?*

Psychological laziness...

This is most efficient kind of laziness. All the challenges of life, all the big decisions, all the difficult choices, are negotiated in the grey matter of your mind. Given up there and your work is done. And that is why perfectionism is the ideal way to never get past the mental starting-block of any goal, project or change.

Giving up is much safer, much easier, too. You don't really have to try.

Low self-esteem

Weighted down with the baggage of self-censure, perfectionists are unhappy, suffer from low self-esteem. Often, they tend to avoid situations, especially competitive situations, that might showcase their presumed imperfections. (This tendency is common even in young children with perfectionistic traits).

In addition, their rigidity, their confrontational attitude and the hyper-critical glasses with which they view the rest of the world tend to isolate perfectionists from others; the alienation and loneliness that result lowers their self-esteem even further.

Part – II
SEVEN STEPS TO HAPPINESS

Chapter - 3

Work with Passion and Zest – Live Life to the Fullest – Be Decisive

"And, what do you do?" That is perhaps the first question that people ask you when you are introduced to them. More often than not, the response is about one's work profile, one's workplace. As though people are known not for who they are, but for who their employer is! However, there are always a few who buck the trend and respond by describing their passion, not their job. These are the people who aren't forgotten before you order the next drink. They redefine 'lifestyle' as 'life in style'…..their style.

Happiness is felt while you are working. It is not something that will happen after work. Our idea is: "I will work, I will get the result, then I will go to the market, buy a few things, enjoy myself, and I will be happy." I can assure you, you will not be happy you will get only some comforts…..you alone can make yourself happy. Therefore don't work for happiness, but work as a happy person. This develops your inner potential.

When you are making a product in the factory let us say stitching shoes or making fabrics, can you change your attitude to work? Can you work as an act of joyous self-expression? Generally we don't understand this truth that work is a means of self-expression and creating dignity for oneself. Lord Krishna says never run away from work *(Bhagvad Gita, III-4): Nahi sanyas na deva siddhim samatigac chati.* Chage your attitude towards work and continue to do your work, you are able to unfold your inner potential. That is freedom. That is happiness. It is that happiness all of us are seeking. The usual state is when we are just asking for gross reward, and a gross result without any regard for satisfaction or happiness. Because a person who just works for an award has no other consideration. The person is going to disintegrate. He will be treated like the silkworm that produces silk around itself. The sericulturist puts the silkworm in boiling water and takes the silk away. Nobody bothers about the worm.

Similarly, if you don't enjoy your work as you are doing it and if you think, "when I get the result I will have enjoyment", you are mistaken. You will be like the silkworm. You keep producing silk, thinking at the end of it you will be happy. In fact, you are encasing yourself in a silken prison if you work 10 or 12, hours a day without passion.

Emotional outlet

There are many who believe that having a passion is not only a great stress-busters, it is also a great companion. Kuchipudi dancer Yamini Reddy feels she is able to live better through poetry. "Whenever I feel a gush of sadness or happiness, I transfer it into a poem in my scrapbook wherever I am, whether in a train or on a flight. By off-loading my feelings on to paper, I feel relaxed and reassured. There are numerous such examples.

"Table Tennis gives me a sense of fulfilment, free of any kind of responsibility. It energizes me for other roles," – says Nana Patekar, the actor.

Lord of the Rings star Viggo Mortensen (Aragon) is an accomplished painter, poet and photographer and has combined his skills to put together several beautiful coffee table books.

Cooking maybe drudgery for some but for legendary entertainer Sammy Davis Jr, it was a passion. Friends and family still remember the lavish meals that he cooked.

Singer Tony Bennett's paintings have sold for thousands of dollars to fellow celebrities like Oprah Winfrey, Carol Burnett, etc.

If you were Amit Burman, CEO, Dabur Foods, racing down the Delhi roads in his favourite car, you perhaps might forget you have seen him in a pin-striped suit negotiating deals worth millions. "I've always been passionate about doing something innovative, be in venturing into the packaged food industry or preparing my favourite cocktail, or acquiring a certified pilot's license. I am totally committed to my work as well as my hobbies."

There is a lot of truth in the old saying that all work and no play makes Jack a dull boy. In today's lifestyle, those with a passion are definitely not dull boys and girls. They're the ones who stand out in a crowd.

As you grow, so should your passion. Find out more about whatever it is that interests you. Read, meet, interact and take it to the next level. The sense of achievement is worth it.

True happiness is hard work

Can instant gratification in the form of a pill equal happiness? The question has arisen not as a result of some idle philosophical thought but in response to the latest stride that science has taken. Scientists are working on medication to block painful and traumatic memories.

If one were to take a short-term view of this, it may seem like a positive development. After all, in the 21st century everything is instant, so why should anyone have to work hard at having to cope with past pain? But however accustomed we may have become to the microwave culture, the bitter truth is that happiness is not like a microwave oven or for that matter even the Internet.

The terms, 'instant gratification' and 'happiness' are *oxymorons*. Fast food may give a quick rush of energy or alcohol can give an instant high if you are feeling low, but the aftereffects of both are worse than what they set out to correct in the first place. Happiness is not an absence of unpleasant turn of events in one's life, but an ability to put them in perspective and move forward using these sad moments as a springboard for future happiness.

While all this may sound like *New Age pop psychology* if one were to look at, say, the way our places of major pilgrimage are located, this point becomes clearer. *Vaishno Devi , Tirupati* are atop hills, and are difficult to access. Yet millions of pilgrims, even those who are physically challenged, make the trip to find *salvation, peace of mind* or to use another word, *find happiness in this lifetime.*

No one will deny that this culture of wanting everything now has harmed rather than helped the human race in the long run. By trying to erase pain from the human mind by just popping a pill, it would further give credence to a wrongly-held belief that life is meant to be just a bed of roses. The truth is, and this cannot be put into a capsule, that life has its share of valleys and peaks and by enhancing our natural coping skills there is nothing one cannot handle.

Flip-flop no more

Being decisive expands our happiness, health and clarity and leaves us feeling energetic and focussed, says life coach. At a time when we have more options than ever, being undecided on something can zap us of our energy. Whether it's planning a day with the family, choosing the right healing approach to follow, buying a house or choosing a partner to spend the rest of our life with, we are faced with indecisiveness and this increases disharmony, frustration, wastes our time while confusing and dissipating creative life force energy. The "perfect decision" is really just a myth.

Why do we suffer from indecision? It's mainly because we think we are inadequate, thinking only of what could go wrong and recalling our failures. Indecisiveness is a fear of consequences.

We pick up this fear during childhood and through our experiences. Indecisiveness is one of the biggest obstructions in our energy field towards our goals and success – spiritual and material. We feel so under pressure to succeed that failing starts even before starting off. The habit of "if I had" or "should have" after making a decision only adds to it.

The past *karma* of many individuals would tell the story of a developed habit of escaping from the torment of indecision by turning to someone else – a spouse, priest, physician or psychiatrist, hoping that they would make the decision for you.

In the Mahabharata, Arjuna was plagued by indecision – should he go ahead with a war in which he would have to kill his relatives? Krishna showed him how it was necessary to take the decision to fulfil his role in his life.

The Bhagvad Gita emphasises that action is superior to inaction. Gautama Buddha stressed the need for individual salvation through self-discipline and action by taking decisions and sticking by them. We will continue to face the same torment repeatedly unless we simplify our lives by taking firm decisions.

Making decisions can expand your happiness, health and clarity and can leave you more energetic and focussed on important things. Decision-making increases self-worth and infuses courage to take risks.

- Being a good decision maker is empowering and makes you happier. People fear that if they don't succeed in something, they would be branded a failure, but by not doing anything, they are already failures. When we are flowing and then we come across indecisiveness, it obstructs our energy field towards our goals.
  Here are some tips to get rid of indecisiveness : Ask these questions before making a decision:
- Will this decision boost me towards an inspiring future or keep me stuck in the past?
- Will it bring long-term fulfilment or short-term gratification? Am I standing in my power or am I trying to please another?

- Am I looking for what is right or what will make me happy?
- Will this decision add to my life force or reduce my energy?
- Will I use this decision as a catalyst to grow and evolve?
- Does this decision empower or dis-empower me?
- Is it an act of self-love or self-sabotage?
- Is it an act of faith or fear?
- Am I choosing from Divinity or my Humanity?

Neither your decision nor mine

Right from the moment we begin the day, until we retire, we are constantly faced with the formidable task of making choices. The choice we make is sometimes influenced by instant gratification, at other times, by sense of responsibility, but quite often, it's nothing more than mere adherence to a routine.

Decision making is not made any easier by the mind that tends to vacillate ever so often. In fact, it could compound the problem. The mind is like a naughty child within that quite often pushes us to the cookie jar to dip in just this one more time. It conjures all sorts of brilliant rational reasons and justifications for that moment's indulgence.

There is also a devilish streak in us that unforgivingly assaults the conscience with strictures that tend to dwarf your self-esteem. Life inevitably becomes a see-saw that alternates between hedonism and virtue, pleasure and pain and between self-castigation and achievement.

Most of the decisions that we make are fraught with short-term implications. And the stakes are not very high as well. An indulgence like eating more cookies may at the most add a few kilos or harden the arteries a bit. It might just advance the occurrence of what is inevitable. Perhaps those extra kilos could pass off as testimony to a life well lived, in one sense.

There are times when we are faced with crunch situations. And the decisions we make could alter the course of not just our lives but also impact the lives of others. As the stakes rise, so does the hesitation. The head and the heart seem to wrestle each other for supremacy. The left brain keeps a strict debit and credit account of every alternative. The right brain pops up with very intuitive suggestions. The ego cautions one about what "the others" will say. The maverick within recommends what seems absurd. Amidst the cacophony, the voice of the soul could get hushed and so remain unheard or unheeded. Repeated attempts to evoke audibility above all the din makes it barely discernible.

The voice of the soul or the inner voice needs amplification. It is a high fidelity source that metes out an optimised option. The voice within is the voice that helps you blend reality with dreams. It harmonises the internal and the external. It is a holistic mix of practicality and possibility. It often gets discounted by seemingly wiser considerations, but isn't wisdom always in retrospect? The rest is speculation. The feeling of being in total control while making a decision is an illusion. This is because our decisions are based largely on circumstances. The circumstances are usually beyond our control ,howsoever powerful one might be.

A decision is essentially a way out of the maze of circumstances. The maze is a construct that is unique in every situation. We certainly cannot design the maze as per our choice. The impact of the situational maze restricts our decision making to very narrow bandwidth of exercising our choice. Free will is restricted to an excursion on this turf restricted by the circumstances. Priding ourselves about our achievements very often is a trespass by our ego of the uncontrolled domain. It might make for a fabulous recipe, but the credit in all probability is not due to the individual or his mind but because of a string of factors and circumstances.

Happiness is Homemade

We are able to perform better when our family life is happy and contended. Regardless of whether we live in the US, India or anywhere else, family is the building block of any society, and our greatest fulfilment lies there. Of course, one needs to give due importance to work. But if any society works diligently in every other area but neglects the family, it would be the same as straightening deck chairs on the Titanic.

We all seek happiness but what most of us discover is that happiness is a homemade product. If you have strong and effective relationship with family members–whether living together or apart–the resultant good vibes and mental solace tend to overflow into all other aspects of life. When your family is heading in the right direction, you are better able to perform and focus at work. On the other hand, if things aren't going well at home, it is difficult to be deeply happy anywhere else. Thus, it is supremely important that at home, with your family, you concentrate on creating a beautiful family culture.

Marriage is more than a contractual relationship–it is a promise from each individual to stay true to their love and commitment. While I can't tell you how to choose the right mate, I can advise you to determine what your values and principles are–and who might be a complimentary companion. Write a personal mission statement, outlining what is important to you, how you envision marriage and what family means to you. When the time is right, share this with your companion and encourage him/her to do the same.

Happy marriages don't just happen – they are created with body, mind, heart and spirit. No one can afford to get lazy in their relationship with their spouse. It must be nurtured and tended to. And when it gets off the track, as all relationships tend to, from time to time, we must correct our course and come back on track.

You will find that going back to your own mission statement can act as the guiding force that brings you back – because you will live according to what matters most to you.

One of the best ways of keeping a marriage and family effective and healthy is by living the 'Seven Habits'. These embody universal, timeless principles–they belong to you, to me and all the people in the world. They are not my creation. You already know these principles because you know them to be true and already exercise them to varying degrees. I have simply put a framework around principles and organised a systematic way of living them. Committing to these principles may help you strengthen your marriage and family ties. Here is a quick overview:

Be proactive

The power to make a difference in your family lies within you. The place to begin is not with other family members, but with yourself. You have the freedom to choose your actions and you have four unique endowments to guide your responses to people, situations and your environment.

Self-awareness

Step outside of yourself and be aware of your motives, thoughts, feelings and you can decide what you need to change.

Imagination

You can envision what you can be and do.

Conscience

Listen to the inward voice that prompts you to do certain things. Develop it.

Independent will

You can choose what you desire to do, and you have the freedom and the power to do it.

Begin with the end in mind

Decide what you desire for yourself and the culture you would like to develop with your family. This vision is more powerful than any problems you may have in the past or present. Write down your vision in a mission statement and clarify your values and principles.

Put first things first

Organise your priorities according to what matters most to you – in alignment with what you envisioned. Make certain your family has four basic systems in place:

- Selecting goals and making family plans;
- Teaching and training at home;
- Communicating and solving problems together;
- Completing tasks and disciplining within the family.

Think win-win

Win-win is mutual benefit. Win-lose is authoritarian – "I'm right and you're wrong; I make the decisions and you lose." In a win-win family culture, difficult decisions can be made but they are not implemented in a way that violates the larger context of thinking win-win. Thinking win-win is at the heart of an effective family culture.

Understand, then be understood

Seek to understand what other family members feel or think – from their frame of reference – by listening with your ears, heart and mind. When you truly understand, then you can better explain your position or ideas. Listening and understanding is the catalyst that makes effectiveness possible.

Synergize

Cooperate and seek third alternatives that neither single family member could come up with on their own. Through a willingness to communicate, to understand and think win-win, family members can solve most difficult problems or create opportunities that could not have been achieved individually.

Sharpen the saw

Renew yourself and your family by taking care of your physical, mental, social and spiritual needs. Do not neglect these important human needs, or you will eventually pay the price. A beautiful family culture can deteriorate unless the batteries that give its power are continually recharged.

India is a beautiful nation with a rich history, traditions and legacy. Your families are at the heart of your nation—Do not neglect your most precious resource. I know with great surety that living principle-centered lives promises to strengthen us individually, in our marriage, our families, in our communities and at our workplaces. Stay true to your path and remember what matters most to you.

Chapter - 4

Change is Constant – Live in the Present

Change is constant

Change is a constant. Even as aging cells in our body die, new ones are taking their place. When all the cells of the body die, would it mean that the body has reached a changeless state? No. We are more than the sum of our cells. The 'dead' body continues to play host to micro-organisms whose home it was for long. With decomposition, the body's constituents reorganise as different states of matter, the molecules merging with the cosmos, only to take another shape, another form – and the cycle continues. Nothing is destroyed forever. It's there, somewhere, reconfiguring in part or whole, here or there, or just circulating anonymously, but undergoing change, nevertheless.

Change is a continuum everywhere and at all times. Change begets change, and so is in perpetual motion. It has been said that you never step twice into the same river. The flow of water ensures that. It's constantly changing, just as you are. For, like the flowing river, you too are not the same person. Your body is not the same; neither are your thoughts. Physically, you are undergoing constant change. The thoughts that run through your mind, your observations, perceptions, attitude, everything is as fluid as the water's flow. The river is not the same and neither are you.

When the Japanese monk in Kyoto announced the popular decision to call the year, 2009 the year of change, he added, after some thought: "However, it is the individual who must change." To qualify this statement, one might say that when we wish for a particular kind of change in an impersonal manner, expecting it to happen through the actions or decisions of others, the chances of it happening are less than if you began working on yourself. Rhonda Byrne writing in The Secret, goes a step further. She says just sending out wilful thoughts for that change to take place will make it happen because the thought reverberates through the cosmos, the law of attraction plays out, and the wish is fulfilled.

The premise of all these views is that we accept that nothing is unchangeable. Since change is in unstable, it makes more sense to embrace it than to offer resistance.

Live in the moment for Happiness

The mind always seeks to deny the Now and to escape from it. In other words, the more you are identified with your mind, the more you suffer. Or you may put it like this: The more you are able to honour and accept the Now, the more you are free of pain, and suffering. You will be free of the egoic mind.

Why does the mind habitually deny or resist the Now? Because it cannot function and remain in control without time, which is past and future, so it perceives the timeless 'Now' as threatening. *Time and mind are in fact, inseparable.* Imagine the earth devoid of human life, inhabited only by plants and animals. Would it still have a past and a future?

The mind to ensure that it remains in control, seek continuously to cover up the present moment with past and future, and so, as the vitality and infinite creative potential of the Being, which is inseparable from the Now, becomes covered up by time, your true nature becomes obscured by the mind.

Always say, 'yes' to the present moment. What could be more futile, more insane, than to create an inner resistance to something that already is? If you no longer want to create pain for yourself and others, if you no longer want to add to the residue of past pain that still lives on in suffering under this burden, but they also keep adding to it every moment whenever they ignore or deny that precious moment or reduce it to a means of getting to some future moment, which only exists in the mind, never in actuality.

Life is a journey–Take note that every moment is an opportunity–Enjoy the journey

Know that all that has gone in your life before this moment has brought you to where you are right now, that there is a purpose for everything that happens. Rejoice in every obstacle you are faced with in your lifetime and that it is both a gift and an opportunity. This will certainly enable you to grow.

Remember that the only thing that stands between you and fulfilment of your heart's desires is your own fears. Start to face the truth and take note that every moment is an opportunity to create a new reality, NOW, and in every moment of your life. Base this on the unlimited possibilities of what can be, not on your fears of what has happened in your past.

Start to understand that your successes and your happiness is limited only by what you believe is possible. The range of possibilities are only restricted by limited human understanding. Trust the universe, it will show you the answers when you are open to receive them.

Now perhaps some of these ideas are new to you, perhaps, you want to reject them as nonsense or as impossible, that is your right. You don't have to accept anything in life or what I say. You have your own free will to reject or accept that there might be something in these ideas, even if it is not clear, right now, what or how or why?

As you continue your journey of enlightenment and self-discovery, you may find some things that made no sense at the time, might then begin to seem possible and perhaps, even probable. What is important is that you apply yourself with an open mind and an open heart. Rejecting everything that is out of your hands just because it does not make sense will not lead to spiritual understanding. Everyone's path is different, so do not assume that what works for someone else will necessarily work for you, or vice versa.

You need to find yourself those things that work for you and those that do not. You will also find the speed of your journey and the timing of events in everyone's lives will vary. It's important not to give yourself a hard time just because events are not happening as quickly as you would like or that your experiences are different from someone else's.

It will certainly get uncomfortable at times, but remember there is no growth without risk and enlightenment cannot work without growth, love, trust, understanding and compassion. You are perfect just the way you are although if you wish to grow in love and light, you need to be prepared to place yourself into situations that will take you to the limits and you may feel uncomfortable.

The fact is that they are only uncomfortable to you, no one else. There maybe times when you need to face up to some unpleasant truths. You have nothing to gain by trying to deceive yourself or others. When you take the easy options, it will not lead to growth and enlightenment. So are you ready to take the risk and to take yourself on?

There are no teachers; you are your own teacher. Just as you would learn from a teacher, you learn from yourself. The two go hand in hand, just as the only way you can receive is for you to give, the only way to be loved is to give love back, and the only way to be forgiven is for you to forgive.

The most important thing to remember is to love, respect and honour and forgive ourselves as well as others. This is a journey, so enjoy the travelling and don't forget to smell the roses on the way.

Find unconditional happiness in the present

In the Bhagavad Gita, Sri Krishna describes how three types of persons, with three different visions live in the world. A person with a *sattwic* vision lives in bliss and freedom because he or she perceives the oneness of things and beings and therefore, the heart is filled with love for all. The *rajasic* person is constantly struggling as he sees differences, which create likes and dislikes in the mind. The *tamasic* person lives in bondage as he takes the part for the whole and gets fanatically attached to one little thing. The majority of people belong to the second category. They are always craving and longing for the results of action. For them, happiness is based on the result of the action. One will agree that we want happiness and we want it now and forever. But, our way of living and thinking is such that we always say, "If I get this object, then I will be happy," or, " I am doing this to get a specific result to be happy." We keep postponing our happiness for the future. Thus man is always preparing himself to be happy – he's never happy!

Now look at the contradiction: I want happiness now but I am keeping it in the future by making it dependent on the result. So firstly, my happiness will be in the future and secondly, since the future is uncertain, my happiness is also uncertain.

But suppose, I enjoy the very action itself, the essential point is that an action is always performed in the present – you cannot perform an action in the past or the future. So if my joy is in the action itself, then my joy is in the present. And since the action is in my hands; it is within my reach, there is no uncertainty about it either.

I have the choice to perform an action, but once the action is performed, the result is not in my control as the result depends on many other factors. For example, I want to win an election. I can do all the necessary arrangements, file the nomination, spend endless hours canvassing for myself, but whether I will win or not, will depend on the votes of the people. Thus, happiness is fleeting, uncertain and in the future for a person obsessed with the results of his actions. Such a person becomes extremely greedy; and his life becomes a relentless and futile struggle for happiness.

How to enjoy the moment

Have you ever in your quest to be more and do more, experienced the feeling that you were going backward? We all seem to be overstretching ourselves. I am always saying, "I never thought life would be this busy". Could all this busyness actually prevent us or be creating blocks in our lives to what we are truly seeking? Could we actually start slowing down and asking ourselves different questions that would end up creating a more profound awareness in our lives? Can this hectic life with so many distractions keep us from a life where we are in appreciation of each and every moment of our day?

We live in a world with so many expectations and so much to accomplish. Financial well-being, relationships that work, looking good and to be everything society wants us to be. Do all these burdens and expectations are actually be causing damage to our well being, to the physical mind and body and in turn slowing the real growth we seek here on this planet? Does this damage that we have possibly caused need to be healed and will we slow down enough to heal ourselves? We pursue all these things to create a place of wholeness. We seek a life that is complete and whole and dream of enjoying all that life has to offer. But do we ever get to the place of peace, calmness, and serenity and do we ever find the love for our lives?

When will we begin to recognise that this is not working? And that we just keep doing more but the wholeness of our lives is just a big hole. Well, there is hope. When we start to recognise what is going on and pay attention, we can take steps in creating and changing our lives to make a difference.

When we recognise that we need to be responsible for our own lives and that we are the ones who ultimately create our reality, we can actually break through all the expectations others have put on us and take the time to enjoy the moment. I am not saying that we just sit around and do nothing. The point that I am making is that we are so busy that we are never where we are. We are doing one task and thinking about the next task. We are in our cars, talking on the phone and thinking about the meeting we have later that day.

We pick up a friend from the airport or we are at lunch with our family and we just have to answer that call from a friend who just wants to chit chat. When does it all slow down? When do we just be with someone or something? Like taking the time to read a book, or just sitting there and listening to your child, without all the noise going on in your head of what you have to do next? How about just being? Breathing and being in that moment from time to time and just enjoying it.

A good friend of mine would sometimes take a Friday afternoon off from work and just be with the day – enjoying the sunshine and feeling the warmth of the sun.

Do you ever slow down and listen to the birds sing, or watch a humming bird hover like a helicopter as it pecks at a bougainvillea? Do you still fell the coolness and that little tickle of the grass on your feet or are you just traversing this planet in pursuit of something you just cannot get your hand around?

Try breathing in and out slowly and feel the air move through your body. Do it now! Appreciate this moment and be in gratitude for this moment. Yes, you can tend to your busy life later, but from time to time stop and just BE.

Be open to seeing and feeling what is going on around you and really appreciate for whatever it offers. Let the world take care of itself for a while. You don't have to always fix everything.

As you get good moment you will learn how to do this even when you are busy. You can take on tasks and just be in that task. You can actually enjoy the task and do it so well that you don't even realise how quickly time has passed and how efficient you were in accomplishing and enjoying that task. You can talk to someone and actually hear what they mean, not just what they are saying. So pay attention every moment of your life.

Pause to connect within

Life has become mechanical and in the rush to do our best at work and in personal relationships, we are losing sight of what we really are. We have also forgotten how to focus. We are often haunted by questions, such as "How can I achieve what I want? What is my life's purpose?" Life is in constant flux and the demands on us in our careers and in the family are constantly changing. We find ourselves constantly preparing for the next, new challenge. The demand can get exhausting and we practically operate on auto-pilot.

Don't look for approval

This statement echoes a regular mother's complaint – "I have to cook for my children, pick and drop them, cater to my husband's need and before I know it, it's time for bed. I don't have time for myself!" A visit to a beauty parlour or an exotic spa over the weekend offers only a temporary escape. As we rush from one task to the next; we are unconsciously seeking approval from those around us.

What makes us dwell in the past or project into the future are our fears, of losing something or someone, being rejected, not being good enough or being betrayed by people we trust. This creates anxiety and builds a super vigilant state where we unquestioningly submit to or tightly control the environment. These fears stem from the past, but we keep it alive by focusing on the event and reminding ourselves of how bad or good it was.

Get some me-time

We are always with ourselves, but do we ever speak to the 'me' the way we do with everyone else? By-making time for ourselves for a few minutes during the day, independent of external circumstances, we can slowly relax and get used to our own presence and eventually extend this comfort to others around us. We must learn to enjoy doing things for ourselves. Here's how to go about it. Choose a quiet place that you love, perhaps a balcony, and look at objects that make you smile. Then, taking a deep breath, stroke your hands with your palm and reassure yourself, "I am safe in my world. I belong to this environment that I lovingly create. I allow myself to flow in this moment. I am grateful to this moment and life". Absorb this feeling with gentleness. The point is to feel and believe what you say.

Take a deep breath and be still. Look at all the things that life has given you. You have received this because you are worth it and have earned it. Acknowledge them today!

Carrying this new energy, we learn to respond to a situation, rather than react impulsively. On a regular schedule, this recharge is possible every 45 minutes with five even cycles of deep breathing in an undisturbed space.

Slowly, over a period of time, we begin to appreciate ourselves in our environment. "I" becomes the most important person and the feeling overpowers whatever we do.

Trust life

This is how to recharge yourself. When we do things that we love, our involvement creates feel-good hormones in sync with the natural body. That is why gardening, playing with children, reading, writing, singing and dancing bring about calmness and refresh the body, mind and environment.

Our life's purpose slowly evolves. Till the time we are on the highway of life, it is important to notice everything that our eyes can see and feel gently, rather than focus on the endless road. We came because we were needed. Life is the driving force taking us ahead. We just need to trust it. When we take in something calmly, we respond differently. And as we continue on the journey of life, we can add our own joy to the situation.

Creating a fresh new energy around us regularly that is tapped by breathing and affirming at regular intervals, can change the way we respond to life. Discovering our purpose is adding value with our feelings that, over a period of time, reveal our uniqueness. When we let go the fears, we are ourselves in the present moment. This needs "you" and "your appreciation" to help you move ahead to the next moment from this beautiful present.

How to live in your current day-to-day life

There is a beautiful verse in the Bhagawad Gita describing the characteristics of a liberated soul and how he lives in freedom. He does not brood over the past nor worry or fear regarding the future. He lives in a kind of detached objectivity in the present.

To understand this clearly let us see how the ignorant man remains bound and enslaved to the past, present and future. When one is in the present, one is constantly reminiscing over past happy memories or grieving over unpleasant ones. As a student having ruined an examination paper I spent the next day brooding over it.

The future is unknown but despite that we continue to fear, fret, and worry over it. We want to know what the future holds. People love to have their horoscopes read; consult palmists, astrologers, and numerologists, all in a bid to overcome the fear of the unknown future so, we brood over the past and fear the future. Moreover, even in the present, we get excited and nervous, and especially when the situation demands some action, we become so confused that we are unable to think objectively. One day it suddenly struck me that the past, present and future in English grammar are all referred to as past tense, present tense, and future tense. We do not say: past relax, present relax, or future relax! This is because when dwelling on the past we become tense; in the present we are tense, we remain tense about the future.

Once, it so happened that a rich man's cook prepared an unpalatable meal. The man was extremely upset and shouted and scolded the cook. The next day, the cook worked hard and prepared a delicious meal. The man ate it and remarked, "Today, the food is very good, but what happened yesterday? Why did I have to suffer? Why didn't you cook like this? Now, promise that tomorrow you will cook the food like this..."

We go through life suffering like the rich man. Without brooding we need to learn lessons from the past, drop it and move ahead. The future is unknown; do not go on developing imaginary fears. Live in the present; be detached without getting excited, nervous, or agitated. Do not live in bondage and slavery, live in freedom and bliss.

Today's world is full of restlessness, restlessness both inside and out. Dissatisfaction is on the rise, a sense of being incomplete. Due to this dissatisfaction, we rarely live in the present. Instead, we spend most of our lives dreaming of the past – the good that was, the good that should have been – or dreaming of the future and the potential happiness waiting for us. Running back and forth between these two poles fuels our disease and ultimately leaves us exhausted.

So much energy is wasted that we could put into enhancing ourselves, our families, our jobs, our society. It only we could realise that the happiness, beauty, satisfaction we were searching for is in "the now".

The benefit of meditation is only to be felt in the time spent sitting with eyes closed. When we practise meditation regularly, it affects all areas of our lives. It centres us, quietens our restless minds, sharpens our intellects, make us more aware of what is going on around us; it opens our hearts to the beauty and bliss of each moment, to the interconnectedness and unity inherent in all beings. The silence we experience in the depth of meditation carries over into the rest of our day, thus calming the noisy mind. With the mind stilled, we find ourselves less irritable and less distracted. The energy normally wasted on unessential thoughts is now available for us to direct, as we deem fit, allowing us to focus more properly on the job at hand.

Chapter - 5

Live Free from Attachment

Freedom from attachment is different from Renunciation

Simply put, happiness is satisfaction of mind. However, different individuals have different perceptions of how to achieve happiness. For some, happiness lies in wealth; for others, it is in rank and position; yet others find happiness in fame and name. Commonly, happiness is measured by achievement in terms of money, property, other material possessions, power, name, fame, education, lifestyle, position and social status.

In their quest for 'happiness', individuals tread a path that destroys the inner good instincts and virtues. Craving for material wealth begets greed and greed leads to corruption. Similar is the outcome when passion for power drives one's mind.

But people fail to see this truth. Individuals are impelled to believe that material achievement is the truth of life; and, in the process, it fuels attachment to worldly pursuits and sensory pleasures. Growing attachment breeds addiction to material attainments. In turn, such addiction intoxicates the human mind, making it oblivious to the truth. So real happiness remains a mirage.

Some may argue that the incentive behind every work is gain, without which an individual will not be motivated to work. Then why the detachment is required at all.

With attachment arises dependence on the object of your attachment and with dependence comes slavery–you are then controlled by your attachment. If the object of your attachment is out of your reach, you become miserable and hanker after it. Then again, if you manage to own it, you are in constant fear of losing it. Thereby your freedom of expression, behavioural patterns and outlook on life become limited.

Let us go beyond 'I'

Why do we have this urge to prove our worth all the time to everyone? Who cares anyway? Have you noticed the increasing use of the 'I' word in conversations around us?

"I did this", "I said that..." Ultimately, I had to resolve the situation..."

When someone goes wrong, "Didn't I warn you beforehand...?"

When someone achieves something, "Oh, I always knew you would win this!"

When something untoward happens, "I did have a premonition..."

And don't just smile and nod in agreement. You do it too! All of us have this deep-seated, all pervasive need to make our mark on events around us. Most conversations end up being nothing but an overlap of "I-s", where each one tries to tell his/her story, or tries to prove his/her point. A long, dissatisfying talk later, you realise all you did was exhaust yourself trying to get your words across the others! Why this urge to prove our worth all the time, with everyone? Why do we need to keep stressing and advertising our ideas, thoughts, dreams, successes, both big and small.

Perhaps the phrase, "pushing your boundaries" or "pushing yourself to perform better" takes on a whole new meaning for us when we try to impose our thoughts and ideas on those around us! Rather than pushing ourselves to perform better and going outside our comfort zone in pursuit of greater success, we think the more noise we make about our accomplishments, the better we become.

But to those who listen carefully, the echo of a hollow 'I' is very clear. A senior colleague enjoys quoting the instance when he interviewed a young executive who spent time convincing him how he was a single-man team at his previous job! "you know what this told me about the guy?" asks the colleague. "So much use of 'I' showed me he was an extremely poor team leader!"

Can we not just be happy as good human beings going about our lives without having to compete with the best?

In a world overpopulated by celebrities, perhaps the need to prove our own worth increases, and easy availability of social media encourages a self-promotional audience to indulge with impunity. Generation Y is certainly all about "I, Me, Myself" and older generations, perhaps see no harm in picking up a bit of the attitude from them. The internet news blog mashable.com quotes a recent survey of college students on attitudes. "Almost 40% (of Gen Y) agree that "being self-promoting, narcissistic, overconfident, and attention seeking is helpful for succeeding in a competitive world!"

There was a time not long back when after a certain age, with a good job in hand and a family around us, we would settle down to stability and comfort. The only bit of promotional indulgence would be to encourage kids to recite a nursery rhyme or sing a song to impress visiting uncles and aunts. Today however, it is not just the kid, but the dad, the mom, the dog and even the house help who all set out to prove their accomplishments. For we are all told we need to keep growing; stopping and resting on your laurels just isn't an option anymore. And so you are subjected to stories about the supposed intellect of kids you know for sure are duffers, and incidents cooked up to prove everyone's superiority to the person next to line.

Where even celebrities and pseudo celebs feel the need for and use all available opportunities to promote themselves, the pressure on ordinary mortals to do likewise becomes immense. So then what happens to those amongst us who want to sit back and take it easy? Those of us who accept that we do not excel in anything to the extent of overshadowing all others! Can we not just be happy as good human beings going about or lives without having to compete with the best? After all, there can be only so many who march ahead and for that, there will have to be others who need to take a backseat. Need taking that seat necessarily mean having lost the race.

A colleague's young life cut short unexpectedly due to immense stress brings home like nothing else the message that we are all running around like headless chickens for nothing! Must all growth and development be outward? Some time ago *The Times of India* dropped the capital 'I' to be replaced by a smaller 'i' on its edit page. Would it be so tough for us to do the same in our daily lives?

Why can we not stop 'I'ing to the outer world and start 'eyeing' our inner selves? For if we shine from within, the peace and contentment will be reflected to rest of the world around us as well.

Even loneliness is lovely – It is a source of love and joy

Loneliness is lovely. The Supreme bestows loneliness on people to provide them with an opportunity to search for their true self and get connected to the Supreme Source of love and joy. In loneliness, you can hear the sounds of true harmony, rhythm and perfection of the Universal design. Use this loneliness to creat something beautiful by developing a hobby that engrosses your whole attention. It maybe reading, painting, gardening, even music. Maybe through your hobby, you will get a friend or co-traveller of your own frequency.

Any time that is 'me' time is a good idea, where one can connect with oneself. It can be anywhere, even in the bathroom or just before sleeping. Physical space, if available, is a boon.

Don't let loneliness depress you. Everything is divine about our true self. And depression is not an illness or disease. It is a plateau given by Nature to know the true meaning and importance of detachment. In the complete life cycle of a human being, plateaus of depression are sure to happen at least seven to ten times at an interval of 8-12 years. When a mentally evolved human finds the world meaningless or shall be say, when the true face of the world becomes visible, to an emotional and sensitive individual, then this state of plateau or 'camp' is created. Mental hurt is not the only reason for it. A break or hindrance in the mental, spiritual and economic growth can also be a reason for this condition.

A human who does some soul searching, meditation and contemplation surfaces through these plateaus or base camps, due to his own will power (soul power) and gets a new life, new energy, and moves forward. However, whosoever indulges in it, gets mentally ill-balanced, can also harm himself, which is sin, an insult to the internal powers of the human. Only the person who goes through depression and emerges as a better human being can contribute towards humanity and is capable of bearing future plateaus.

Depression is just a plateau, a base camp to reach the topmost, highest peak. You cannot reach the top of the peak in one breath; you will break, disintegrate on the way. Learn how to move, forward with enthusiasm after complete rest and preparation at these base camps. So loneliness is not to be shunned, but utilised for growth – and for knowing thy true self. That is the only way. The journey never ends, and simultaneously we can fulfil our worldly duties along with inner growth. Nothing is to be renounced, for we just need to know how to sail through it peacefully, gracefully and with our entire might to slowly become wiser and more at ease and at peace with our own self.

Everything happening in life is there to propel us towards growth and transformation. A human being has all the potential to perceive and derive positivity from every condition. Me, My self, My God, My Soul And My Tranquillity, I am Five, I am not alone.

Detachment ss. attachment – Detachment gives us freedom of thought which is a source of joy

With attachment arises the idea of possession, the sense of ownership, such as, my house, my car, my family, my wealth, etc. This sense of ownership is an outcome of a lower ego. With each new possession your ego is reinforced, until finally your possessions, begin to dominate and control your life. Imagine an enormous man who is chained to the ground. There seems to be no escape. This is how we are chained to the objects of our attachment.

Surveying the happenings in your country and the world over, it is not difficult to guess why the world is getting deeper into a quagmire of chaos and confusion. The crisis of culture and the emphasis on economy and technology as a first priority has isolated the individual from his ecological environment. The present day society incites individuals to become more self-centred and achievement-oriented.

This kind of social system encourages competitive relations. The struggle to nurture an idealised self-image in competitive relationships diminishes our tolerance of failure. Being unable to accept this failure, one sees various ways to escape an essential moral dilemma.

The desire for adventure and the quest for novel experiences in a dull or indifferent social climate of purposelessness are yet other factors leading the youth of today to substance abuse. Some use drugs, some seek recourse to "packaged spirituality", some to various forms of vulgarity, for combating boredom and depression, or to cope with a sense of alienation and disillusionment they experience in relation to social norms and values.

In order to be detached, you do not have to renounce everything? Not at all. We often imagine that a person who is detached will be indifferent to those around him and dislike everything that reminds him of what he has renounced. This is not true. Detachment is only possible for those who remain unaffected or undisturbed by every situation in life. Only the person who is able to maintain equipoise and balance in the face of success and failure, love and hatred, pain and pleasure, is truly detached.

Detachment, on the other hand, develops freedom of thought, word and deed. It frees you from the fetters which bind you to the ordinary plane of awareness. One who is detached may enjoy every pleasure of life, acquire wealth and status, raise a family that he loves, control a vast business, or even an empire. On account of his detachment, however, he is never dependent on them. He enjoys everything, but as the master and not the slave. On account of his detachment, he develops an inner freedom or independence which nothing can conquer. No adversity can shatter him, because he remains unaffected, and no amount of success can affect him, for he is established in equanimity. Thereby he becomes the master of himself in every situation.

Detachment, therefore, should be understood as the ability to remain unaffected in the face of the trials and tribulations of life. With detachment comes a greater feeling of love and unity with those around you.

We all honour men and women of courage. What prevents people from showing courage in their own lives? Purely and simply, it is their attachments. The fear of losing what they have, defined by them in their hearts as their security. *Nothing in the world is secure. Life itself will be stripped from you someday, perhaps, at a moment's notice, or even with no notice at all.*

You will find it helpful to keep in mind that security lies in yourself, not in anything outside.

Chapter - 6

Good Health – You can Stall Ageing and Remain Happy

A calmer, smarter and happier you

You can use your workouts to train your brain. Exercise improves your memory, creativity and decision-making ability. Forget about a better body workout to a better you. A brainstorm, a brilliant flash of insight, an elusive solution to a problem that's been bothering you. What is it about sweat that lubricates your mental muscle and makes such breakthroughs possible? Researchers have long known that cardio workouts kick up levels of feel-good chemicals in the brain, including the neurotransmitters known as endorphins, which decrease stress. But evidence from research done over the past 5 to 6 years indicates that the reason these exercise-induced brain changes help you achieve cerebral stunts of extraordinary clarity is that they may allow emotional distractions to fall away. "It's hard to be creative, much less think straight, when you're emotionally overwhelmed," says Frank Perna, Ph.D., an Associate Professor and Director of Health Psychology at the Boston University School of Medicine. "You may already know the solution to your problem, but you're too distracted, emotionally and cognitively, to address it. Exercise allows you to refocus, so your mind takes the centrestage."

Even better, other research reveals that exercise speeds blood flow to the brain, particularly to the right hemisphere, which is associated with creativity and imagination. "Your brain requires nutrients to perform most efficiently, and oxygen-rich blood maybe the key," says Perna. "Exercise has been shown to boost memory, concentration and reaction time," says Psychology Professor Arthur F. Kramer of the University of Illinois.

And the best reason of all: Exercise – the aerobic kind may boost your brain over the long term as well. The latest results from the University of Illinois study indicate that three hours of aerobic exercise may actually help increase your brain volume (viz. new neurons) and white matter (dendrites connecting neurons which contribute to attention and memory procession) in older adults. In effect 60-plusers who exercised had the brain volumes of people 2 to 3 years younger, in the study.

Many of us already embrace our sweat sessions like modern day oracles, running, hiking and Downward Dog-ing to arrive at a solutions to office conflicts, ruptured relationships, even mundane issues like dinner menus. But what we don't know is how to maximise these mental workouts, how to make the most of these meetings with ourselves. Get more from your meditation in motion with these mental-muscles-building strategies.

Choose cardio to get creative

The more repetitive and rhythmic the workout, the better for your mind, says Psychotherapist Connie Tyne, Executive Director of the Cooper Wellness Program in Dallas. Activities such as running, walking, swimming and biking don't require conscious direction, an instructor or fancy choreography, so your mind is free to do whatever it pleases. More intense workouts, such as kickboxing can also knock you into a productive mental place because they burn off build-up tension and aggression, says Peter C. Siegel, a sports hypnotherapist who works with professional athletes in Marina Del Rey, California.

The bottom line? "Choose an activity you find meaningful and satisfying," recommends Trent A Petrie, Director of the Centre for Sport Psychology and Performance Excellence at the University of North Texas in Denton. Your exercise time will most likely set the stage for thinking about issues you find important.

Synchronise your sweat session

Phew! Fortunately, the number of miles you log doesn't dictate the number of epiphanies you'll have. In fact, research published in *The Journal of Sport & Exercise Psychology* showed that workouts as brief as 20 minutes can have a profound effect, elevating mood and reducing tension and anger. Another study from the University if Illinois in Urbana-Champaign showed that 45 minutes of rapid walking three times a week can improve your ability to reason and make decisions. Even better, Perna and other experts believe mental agility isn't something you have to train hard to achieve: According to researchers at Nihon Fukushi University in Aichi, Japan, a 30 minute session two to three times a week can strengthen your thinking and make breakthroughs happen.

The catch: How long it takes to hit the cerebral sweet spot differs from everyone, says Juel Bedford, Director of Physical Education at Baraka Health and Wellness, a personal-training company in New York City. "You need to access this zone of peak mental clarity – and the then stay in it. Luckily, this is a skill that you can actually develop.

Plan ahead

"Before you start your workout, decide which muscles you're going to train and which moves you're going to sweat through," says Siegel. "That way, you don't waste precious mental energy trying to organise your circuit while you're in the middle of your sweat session."

Hard day's night

Our body clock holds many secrets. It is probably our best timekeeper, if we simply pay attention to the way it ticks. At dawn our blood pressure experiences its sharpest rise, in readiness for the day's activities. Around lunch time, the liver enzymes kick into full gear in anticipation of food. In the evening, the pineal gland in the base of our brain begins producing the hormone melatonin, which makes us feel sleepy. As we sleep, our body temperature drops. In the morning, as the sun comes up and light hits our retinas, our body stops making melatonin and our temperature rises, reviving up our metabolism for the day ahead.

Working at night impacts the health

Working through the night results in erratic sleep and food timings, which impacts the body clock and the health adversely. Experts say those on night shifts have a fragmented nature of sleep. Even though they sleep for four to five hours during the day, this cannot make up for the sleep deprivation experienced generally. This may lead to sleep walking, lower brain activity, stress, and mood swings. It is not surprising that many night shift workers report falling asleep on the job. According to US National Sleep Foundation, 65 per cent of people on night shifts are sleep deprived, reducing their efficiency, leading them to making more mistakes, and becoming forgetful. These negative effects lead to lower job productivity and can cause accidents. Those who work through the night and are sleep deprived experience more stomach problems, menstrual irregularities, colds, flu and weight gain than day workers. Heart problems are more likely too, along with higher blood pressure and diabetes.

Devanuj Chakrabarty, 24 years old IT professional, has to

work on night shift starting from 7 pm till 4 am for three weeks before two weeks of morning shifts. Erratic food and sleeping schedules, lack of sunshine and almost no social activity have affected his health aversely. "My sleep schedule has gone for a toss. Even when I get to bed on time, I suffer from *insomnia.* When I do fall asleep, I sleep walk. In fact, its scary to recall that I caught myself sleep walking twice in the last month. Once I was sitting on the stairs and another time I was drinking water. Since I am not used to sunlight now, it almost hurts my eyes whenever I go out during the day," he says.

Though those on night shifts have no other option but to report on duty, there is a growing trible of youngsters who are hooked on to TV or the Internet and choose to hit the sack only in the wee hours of the morning. Arijit Sen is one such person, who has not got into bed before 4 am for the past eight years. Addicted to Internet, he uses the no-tariff time period from 10.00 band service provider to download movies and songs. "I started studying at night during my Class X exams and it is now a habit. This robs me off the normal eight hours of sleep needed and I suffer from irritability and fatigue all day. Trying to sleep early is a lost cause since I always end up being online," he says.

Eating disorders are common

Those who work through the night also have a higher incidence of eating disorders, and are either overweight or underweight.

Omar Shah, a call centre employee, gained lots of weight and also suffered from gastrointestinal problems when he began working different shifts in his new job. "It was very tough for my body to adjust. I was skipping meals and gorging myself with junk food. I also started falling sick very often," he says.

In fact, researchers have even established a deeper link between the biological clock and fatty foods. A high fat diet puts biological clocks out of synch, which explains why we eat at times when we should have been resting.

Besides the usual night own syndrome, there are people for whom travelling is part of life. Moving from one time zone to another, they suffer from *jet lag* resulting in *fatigue, disorientation, insomnia* and *upset tummies.* Dislocated and deadened, the sleep-starved traveller wanders through meetings or tourist sites in a haze.

Dr. Balwant Singh, Regional Director of 'Save the Children UK', has been travelling non-stop for the last 18 years and is out of the city for three weeks a month. Sluggish metablism was the first indication that his biological clock was awry. "I suffered from indigestion for a long time due to erratic food. The condition accentuated since I had to make do with different cuisines while on travel. Lack of sleep also led to fatigue and disorientation at times," he confesses.

How you can slow down the ageing process?

The good news is that you can delay ageing by staying healthy. Ageing has little to do with genetics or years and much to do with exercise, diet, lifestyle, choices, behaviour, habits and beliefs. Some people maximise their time, genetics and potential optimally, while others throw it all down the drain and then hope that the doctor will "fix them" as they age. Eating fresh, wholesome foods like fruits, vegetables, whole grains and lean proteins is a fairly common recipe among most nutritional experts. Avoiding excesses of alcohol, smoking, sugar and caffeine are recommendations for staying young and healthy. Regular exercise-whether it's engaging in a sport, going to gym or a daily walk – keeps our bodies supple and energetic. "Without some kind of regular activity, the muscles will waste, lung capacity will decrease, heart will get weaker, and bones will become more brittle," says Dr. Gupta. Flexibility and mobility will decrease, reaction time will slow down, our responses will suffer, making us more susceptible to illnesses and diseases.

Young at heart

Many of us feel younger than we actually are. This perception can actually impact our physical bodies too. "If you accept the attitude that you are only as young as you feel, you will act younger, feel younger, and therefore, look younger. Your attitude will be upbeat and modern as you stay abreast of current trends, adapt to changes in technology, and keep up with the "younger" generation. Your thoughts can keep you young," feels Dr. Rachna Singh, Psychologist, Artemis Hospital. Some psychologists are of the opinion that there is a 'golden age' that people tend to get stuck at as they perceived this to be the best time of their lives. Older people tend to feel about 13 years younger than their chronological age, a new study published in the *Journals of Gerontology: Psychological Science* finds. The seniors in the study, all 70 and over, also thought they looked about 10 years younger than their numerical age, with women perceiving their appearances to be closer to their actual age than men. "People generally felt younger than they actually were, and they also showed relatively high levels of satisfaction with ageing over the time period studied," said researcher Jacqui Smith, a psychologist at the University of Michigan Institute for Social Research. The researchers believe that feeling about 13 years younger is an optimal illusion in old age and helps the elderly stay happy and active. Adapting to new terminology can also keep us younger longer. This involves giving up archaic phrases from our youth, and interacting with the younger generation. "Emotionally stay young at heart by releasing rigidity, going with the flow, and following your passions. Youthfulness is about being adaptable, learning new ways of doing things, and being open to change," says Dr. Singh.

Recently, Japanese scientists have found a way to prevent age related deterioration in the hearts. The gene that is involved in the insulin signalling system which helps regulate the lifespan of cells in the heart was suppressed, resulting in better cardiac function and other biological markers of ageing. The scientists believe that this could help control degeneration of the heart in humans and keep it healthy for a longer time. " To stay youthful, you need a strong blood circulation and to prevent nerve degeneration too, so just keeping the heart healthy is not enough to stay young, but it is definitely a good thing," says Dr. Rakesh Gupta, Senior Consultant Internal Medicine, Apollo Hospital.

Get enough sleep

Indians are not getting enough sleep. A good night's slumber is more important to your health than you may realise. But getting the sleep needed for the body isn't easy. "I hardly got any sleep that night," Shah recalls. The time change had completely disrupted his sleep pattern, and he wasn't rested when he got out of bed at 7 am to get to work. At the office, he could barely concentrate on his work.

Shah wasn't aware just how tired he was until he'd driven a quarter of the 24 kilometres route back to his home in the suburbs. He halted at a busy signal on the way, but fell asleep suddenly at the wheel. He woke up dazed after the motorist behind him honked. Shah drove on, out feeling he couldn't concentrate, soon decided to pull off the main road and found a quiet place to park. He then rolled down the windows a bit and managed to take a two-hour nap in his car. After that Shah could drive home safely.

There's no question that not getting enough sleep can lead to difficulty in concentrating, say sleep disorder experts. In fact, many experts think lack of sleep is the reason for many ailments.

A study paper on sleep disorders by Dr. Kumar Menon and his colleagues, presented at a Bombay (Mumbai) Hospital research seminar, emphasises early detection of the problem and concludes that it is time all physicians "wake up to sleep disorders and include sleep history in evaluating their patients."

Whether the cause is *jet lag, shift work, chronic insomnia,* a sleep disorder or simply trying to put in extra hours at work, we've all experienced the exhaustion caused by lack of sleep. In fact, *sleep is as important to a healthy lifestyle as eating properly and exercising.* Getting a good night's sleep is one of the simplest things you can do to stay healthy.

How much sleep do you need?

A good night's sleep means waking up rested and energised. On an average, a healthy adult requires just over eight hours of sleep a night, according to Dr. Jeffrey Lipsitz, a Canadian expert on sleep disorder.

However, the amount of sleep it takes to achieve rejuvenation varies from person to person "It's not a fixed number," says Joseph De Koninck, a Professor of Psychology, adding that if you consistently get less than you need, "a sleep deficit accumulates."

The time it takes for a sleep deficit to accrue depends on how consistent the problem is, says psychiatrist Robert Levitan. "Missing a couple of hours of sleep every night for a week is probably enough."

How one may have trouble sleeping?

Satish Polekar of Hyderabad knows he doesn't get enough sleep. "I haven't had more than four to five hours of sleep for the last three years," says the 28 years old IIM graduate and Assistant Manager at a BPO. "There's always so much that needs to be done in my professional as well as personal life that I'm constantly thinking."

"All that is stressful," says Polekar. "Although I know I have high energy levels, I'm often tired and drink several cups of coffee to counter the fatigue, but I know I'll be able to concentrate better if only I got more sleep."

A US study found that, at least one-third of adults have significant sleep loss ($6\text{-}1/2$ hours or less of sleep a night). And a recent AC Nielsen poll shows that 29 percent of Indians went to sleep only after midnight and 61 percent slept for seven hours or less. The poll also found Indians to be among the world's earliest risers, with 64 percent getting out of bed before 7 am. (Rising early becomes good only if you also went to bed early).

Why is the modern world so sleep deprived? "We're so busy that we often don't allow enough time for sleep," says Dr. S.R. Dong, a sleep expert, who believes lifestyle is the main factor contributing to lack of sleep. According to the ACNielsen poll, Indians allow family or children to dictate sleep hours more than any other country in the Asia-Pacific region. Though work and habit still dictate sleeping hours across the region, the family centric culture of Indians is an unmistakable determinant of when they rest and for how long, explains an ACNielsen executive.

So does your kids, homework, or your husband's favourite late-night show keep you also awake?

Whether it's rushing to get the housework done, once the kids have gone to bed, attending a social function or working late, we're sleeping less than we should. About 40 per cent of people report trouble sleeping when they're severely pressed for time.

For some, the problem lies not in finding the time to sleep, but in their inability to fall asleep and stay that way. Sleep disorders, including insomnia and *sleep apnoea*, are often the culprit. Actual figures are not available, but it's estimated that tens of millions of adult Indians suffer from insomnia, and an even greater number from sleep disturbances.

How important is a Good Night is Sleep?

Sleep is crucial to maintaining your health. Without it, you increase your susceptibility to an astonishing array of health problems, including heart disease, stroke, diabetes, obesity and depression.

No sleeping enough can compromise your immune system, says Stanley Coren, author of *Sleep Thieves* and a Professor of Psychology. You eat well and exercise in order to keep your immune system up, explains Coren, but if you aren't sleeping, you undo all that good work. "The immune system works best when you're asleep," he says. "That's when your natural killer cells are generated." Natural killer cells are produced in the bone marrow and found in the blood and lymph fluid.

"Natural killer cells are part of the body's defence mechanism against viruses, bacteria, even cancer and they do not work properly in the sleep deprived," says Dong. A study in Turkey found that after 24 hours of sleep deprivation, the percentage of natural killer cells in the blood declined by 37 per cent. Another US study of 23 males found that one night of partial sleep deprivation reduced the natural-killer-cell activity to 72 percent of normal levels. Though their activity returns to normal when we begin to get proper sleep, Coren cautions that "the real problem is that a lot of damage might have been done to your body when your immune system left you undefended and susceptible to infection."

It's not just your immune system that suffers when you cut down on sleep. "There is a higher rate of heart failure among people with sleep disorders and sleep disturbances," says Dr. Micael Sole, a Canadian cardiologist. According to Sole, there is increased evidence of C-reactive protein, an indicator of heart disease risk, in people suffering from sleep loss.

Sleep loss can affect key hormones

Researchers at the University of Chicago discovered that chronic sleep loss can reduce the body's ability to regulate hormones and process carbohydrates. In their study, they reduced the participants' sleep from eight to four hours a night. After less than a week, they noted changes in the body similar to the effects of early diabetes or advanced aging. "Sleep disturbances increase the likelihood of a pre-diabetic state (glucose intolerance and insulin resistance) and obesity," says Sole. Both resistance to insulin and glucose intolerance are also makers for heart disease.

Dietician Ramona Josephson notes that insufficient sleep may affect three hormones that can contribute to obesity. There's a decrease in leptin, the appetite-suppressing hormone found in our fat tissue, she says. Ghrelin, the hormone controlling hunger pangs, increases with lack of sleep, causing greater feelings of hunger. And our bodies produce more of the stress hormone cortisol, which increases fat storage. Not only do the increased hormones resulting from sleep loss make us eat more, but most of us also make poor food choices when we're tired. "The less you sleep, the more your chances of obesity," Josephson says.

How to get a Good Night's Sleep?

- Make sure your room is quiet and dark and your bed is comfortable.
- Get up and go to bed at the same time every day.
- Limit your caffeine consumption and nicotine use. And eat dinner at least two to three hours before bedtime – it's more difficult to fall asleep if your body is still breaking down the food you ate. A light snack just before bed time,

however, maybe helpful.
- Exercise regularly. Physical activity done early in the day may promote deeper, better quality sleep. Too-vigorous exercise just before bedtime, however, may delay sleep.
- "Don't toss and turn for longer than half an hour: Get up and do something calming, such as reading.
- Develop a relaxing pre-sleep ritual, like have a glass of warm milk.
- Get treatment for any medical problems that may contribute to sleep troubles, such as sleep apnoea ad restless leg syndrome. If you still have trouble sleeping, there are a variety of sleep aids available. Though sleeping pills are significantly safer than they used to be, "even the drug companies will tell you that they're not for use in chronic insomnia because they won't make you a better sleeper. They may help you fall asleep on the nights that you take them, but you can develop a tolerance to them," says Lisitz. They are, however, safe for short-term use since they are less addictive than in the past, and they clear the body more quickly. "The most appropriate use of sleeping pills is for situational insomnia: a person who normally sleeps well develops insomnia because of an acute stress," Dong says. B*ut insomnia that lasts for more than a few weeks may signal the presence of a more serious problem.* It's a good idea to consult your doctor before taking any kind of sleeping aid.
- Try Yoga, or consult a good yoga teacher.

Chapter - 7

Be Patient and Calm which will Lead to Happiness

Turn setbacks around by being calm and composed

Swami Vivekananda was a man of great wisdom. He was mature enough to meet any challenge that came before him, however serious it might have been. One of his stories is worth quoting.

His Christian friend, intending to test the Swami's mettle, invited him to his house where he seated him in a room, opposite a table on which lay piled, one on top of the other, sacred books of major world religions. They were placed in such an order that the *Bhagavad Gita* was at the bottom and the *Bible* was right on top. Would Vivekananda get provoked, the host wondered.

But before his guest could say anything, the host pointed towards the books and asked: "Swamiji what is your comment on his arrangement?" *Swamiji smiled gently and said: "The foundation is really good."*

Austrian psychologist, Alfred Adler, in his book, *Individual Psychology*, wrote that he observed humanity all his life and found a unique and special quality in both men and women: *their ability to turn a minus into a plus.* The above incident in which Swami Vivekananda turned a potentially unpleasant situation to good account, is an apt illustration of this principle. It is a fine example of how it is possible to turn a potentially inflammatory situation into a favourable one; one could extend this principle to deriving success from what seems like failure; to meet a challenge by using God-given wisdom.

Potentially, all of us have this unique capacity. But to turn this potential into reality, another quality is required and that is **patience**. *It is patience that makes you turn your potential into reality. Without patience, miracles cannot be performed.*

Being patient means having a calm nature. When you are calm, you can serenely face any challenge without allowing yourself to be provoked, making yourself strong enough to overcome all difficulties. Emotionally unshaken, you are able to develop the capacity for unbiased thinking. Only patience will enable you to use your mental capacity to the fullest extent, so that you maybe able to perform miracles.

Our world is one of provocation. Whenever there are provocations, big or small, you have only two options: either to succumb to anger and hatred and fail to do anything positive in the situation, or to remain patient. *But being patient, you save time and energy.*

Patience is a precious virtue; it costs nothing to acquire this virtue. It requires only the training of your mind; you have to train yourself to control your emotions. This is the most important aspect of this successful formula.

Through patience, you can turn your fortune around; without patience, you can expect nothing but failure. The kind of problems you face are not important. What is important is how you choose to tackle them. The result is in your hand. If you become impatient, you will be a failure, but if you are patient, you have the chance of registering your name in the list of super-achievers.

To feel better, you need to think better

Here is a classic story with a twist: a travelling salesman has a puncture on a dark, lonely road and then discovers he has no jack. He sees a light in a farmhouse. As he walks towards it, his mind churns: "Suppose no one comes to the door." "Suppose they don't have a jack." "Suppose they wont lend me their jack even if they have one." The harder his mind works, the more agitated he becomes, and when the door opens, he punches the farmer and shouts, *"Keep your stupid jack!"*

The story brings a smile, because it pokes fun at a common type of self-defeatist thinking. How often have you heard yourself say. "Nothing *ever* goes the way I planned." I'll *never* make that deadline." "I *always* mess things up."

Such inner speech shapes your actions more than any other single force. Like it or not, you travel through life with your thoughts as navigator. If those thoughts spell doom, that's where you are heading, because negative words sabotage confidence instead of offering support and encouragement.

Simply put, to feel better, you need to think better. Here's how:

1. **Tune in to your thoughts** – The first thing Sue said to her new therapist was, "I know you can't help me, Doctor. I am a complete mess. I keep making mistakes at work, and I am sure I am going to be dismissed. Only yesterday, my boss told me I was being transferred. He called it a promotion. But if I was doing a good job, why transfer me?"

   Then, gradually, Sue's story unfolded. She had received her MBA two years before and was earning an excellent salary. That didn't sound like failure.

   At the end of their first meeting, Sue's therapist told her to jot down her thoughts, particularly at night, if she was having trouble falling asleep. At her next appointment, Sue's list included: "I am not really smart. I got ahead by a series of flukes." "Tomorrow will be a disaster. I have never chaired a meeting before." "My boss looked furious this morning. What did I do?"

   She admitted, "in one day alone, I listed 26 negative thoughts. No wonder I am always tired and depressed." Hearing her fears and forebodings read out loud made Sue realise how much energy she was squandering on imagined catastrophes. It you have been feeling down, it could be you are sending yourself negative messages too. Listen to the words churning inside your head. Repeat them aloud or write them down, if that will help capture them.

   With practice, tuning in will become automatic. As you are walking or driving down the street, you can hear your silent broadcast. Soon your thoughts will do your bidding, rather than the other way around. And when that happens your feelings and actions will change too.

2. **Isolate destructive words and phrases** – Fran's inner voice kept telling her she was "only a secretary." Mark's reminded him he was "just a salesman." With the word *only or just,* they were downgrading their jobs and, by extension, themselves.

   By isolating negative words and phrases, you can pin-point the damage you are doing to yourself. For Fran and Mark, the culprits were *only and just.* Once those words are eliminated, there is nothing destructive about saying, "I am a salesman" or I am a secretary." Both statements open door to positive follow-ups, such "I am on my way up the ladder."

3. **Stop the thought** – Short circuit negative messages as soon as they start by using the one word command *stop!*

"What will I do if...?" *Stop!* In theory, stopping is a simple technique. In practice, it is not as easy as it sounds. To be effective at stopping, you have to be forceful and tenacious. Raise your voice when you give the command. Picture yourself drowning out the inner voice of fear.

Vincent, a hard working bachelor in his just 20s, was an executive in a large company. His mother died when he was young, and his father raised him. They got along well, but his father was overprotective, filling Vincent's head with worrisome thoughts. Without realising it, Vincent carried these thoughts into his adult life. His inner voice had taken over his father's role. Vincent was a worrier.

Although attracted to a woman in his department, he never asked her for a date. His worries immobilised him. "It is not a good idea to date a co-worker," or, "If she says no, I will be embarrassing." When Vincent stopped his inner voice and asked the woman out, she said, "Vincent, what took you so long?"

4. **Accentuate the positive** – There is a story about a man who went to a psychiatrist. "What is the trouble?" asked the doctor.

"Two months ago, my grandfather died and left me $75,000. After a month a cousin passed away and left me $100,000."

"Then why are you depressed?"

"This month, *nothing!*"

When a person is in a depressed mood, everything can seem depressing. So once you have exercised the demons by calling a stop, replace them with good thoughts.

One person described the process this way: "Every night, I used to lie awake with a whirlpool of thoughts spinning in my head: "Was I too harsh with the children?" "Did I forget to return that client's call?"

"Finally, when I was at my wits' end, I thought about the wonderful day with Jenny at the zoo. I recalled how she laughed at the chimps. Soon my head was filled with pleasant memories, and I fell asleep."

Be ready with a thought you have prepared in advance. Think about the promotion you got or a pleasant hike in the woods. In the words of the Bible: "...Whatever is honourable... whatever is lovely, whatever is gracious...think about these things."

5. **Reorient yourself** — Have you ever felt low late in the day, when someone suddenly said, "Let's go out?" Remember how your spirits picked up? You changed the direction of your thinking, and your mood brightened.

   Try it now. You are tense because you must finish a project by Friday. On Saturday, you plan to go shopping with friends. In your mind, replace, "Friday's workload with "Saturdays fun." Practise this technique of going from painful anxiety to an active, problem-solving framework. If flying frightens you, get absorbed in the pattern of lights and roads near the airport as your plane is taking off or landing. During the flight think about some activity on the ground that distracts you.

   By re-orientating, you can learn to see yourself and the world around you differently. If you think you can do something, you increase your chances of doing it. Optimism gets you moving. Depressing thoughts bog you down, because you are thinking. "What's the use?"

   Make it a habit to remember your best self, the you that you want to be. In particular, remember things for which you have been complimented. That is the real you. Make this the frame of reference for your life – a picture of you at your best.

   You will find that re-orientating works like a magnet. Imagine yourself reaching your goals, and your will feel the tug of the magnet pulling you towards them.

   Over the years, we have discovered that when people *think differently*, they *feel* – and *act* – *differently*. It is all in controlling your thoughts. As the poet, John Milton wrote: "The mind...can make a heaven of hell, a hell of heaven."

   The choice is yours.

Chapter - 8

Love and Cheer up in Your Day-to-Day Life

What is Love?

How do we define love? What does it mean to love someone? When we love someone, we desire his/her happiness. Do I desire my own happiness? Well of course I do, at least on first reaction basis. I obviously don't desire my unhappiness. But do I follow up on it? It is one thing to say that one loves someone and desire their happiness. But when we have to make choices that prove us truthful or not, we have to assess how we are successful in this effort.

Many times I wonder, why do we say, "falling in love" rather than saying "rising in love". The obvious answer as it appears to me is that we "fall in love" because love implies total surrender. Unless we surrender our ego to the person we love, we cannot realise the power of "love".

There are two basic emotions in every human being—*love and hate*. All our relationships are affected in some way or the other by these emotions. Love is a very powerful force that holds us together—personal love, family love, country's love are its different manifestations which can bring powerful feelings within us. Selfless love has been exalted down the ages. Physical love which flows out of attachment to a given object ends when the object itself dies. That love cannot be everlasting. *Love is the energy which helps us heal whether we give this love to ourselves or receive it from another,* says motivator and international author, Wayne Dyer.

When we love someone or some cause, we are prepared to sacrifice anything for that person or that cause. In that context what does loving oneself imply? *To me that means to discover yourself.* We come to this world to experience our own reality, to learn who we are and what would be best for us. A time comes in our lives when we are not content with doing the same thing again and again always. Although we may realise it, yet we go on the same way until we die discontented. This is not the way life was intended to be. Life is intended to be lives of joy and wisdom with energy abounding. Generally, we are following someone else's mandate or beliefs. The ideal thing is that we should look deeper inside ourselves and discover where our joy is dormant. Look until you find the things which bring you joy and then begin doing them. This may not happen immediately. It usually takes years for one to open full to oneself after prolonged self-denials. This is the time to seek ourselves in the external world. Our truths are within us. You must go into the new reality which maybe unknown and possibly a little frightening. As Joan Marques, the noted author, has said that many of us are now at the place where we have no alternative but to be true to ourselves. Do not worry if some of the things you are still doing, you do not feel entirely enlightened. As you become more aligned with your truth, you become happier with your life and your life comes more into balance. Only you can know why you are here and can learn to be happy. No one outside you have any of the answers you seek.

In his discourses, Osho exhorts us to nourish our beings with positive feelings and embrace life with gratefulness and gratitude. This is the secret of the art of living—and living consciously. The art of living needs a conscious choice. It is not about drifting unconsciously in all directions. One is not as weak as one starts assuming in a state of misery. One carries within oneself a vast treasure of Godliness. One has to tap it. And the art of tapping is what meditation is all about. Then life becomes a celebration, a carnival of joys.

Life has been given to you to create, to rejoice and to celebrate. When life is easy, comfortable, convenient, who cares? Who bothers? You have loved someone and then one day that person is gone. Crying in your loneliness, that is the occasion you can become aware. The pain is not to make you miserable, the pain is to make you more aware and when you are aware, misery disappears.

Love 24X7 takes you to the state of everlasting joy

Four important subjects are discussed in the *Samiddhi Sutra:* the idea of happiness, the existence of real joy, the practice of reliance, and the trap of complexes. Our notions about happiness entrap us. We forget that they are just ideas. Our ideas of happiness can prevent us from actually being happy.

The second idea is that of the existence of real joy. When a Goddess asked the young monk, Samiddhi why he chose to abandon happiness in the present moment for a vague promise of happiness in the future, Samiddhi answered: "The opposite is true. It is the idea of happiness in the future that I have abandoned, so I can dwell deeply in the present moment."

The third topic, the *Sutra* discusses is the practice of reliance, or support. Relying on *Dharma* is not just an idea. When you live in accordance with the *Dharma*, you realise *joy, tranquillity, stability, and freedom*. It is "taking refuge in the island of self," the island of peace in each of us. We must know how to return to that island when we need to. In his last moments, the Buddha said: "Take refuge in the island of the *self*...There you will find B*uddha, Dharma,* and *Sangha".*

The fourth subject concerns the trap of complexes – thinking you are better, worse than, or equal to others. The complexes arise because we think we are a separate self. Happiness built on the notion of a separate self is weak and unreliable. Through the practice of meditation, we come to see that we "inter-are" with all other beings, and our fears, anxieties, anger and sorrow disappear. If you practise true happiness, relying on the Dharma and realising the interconnected and interdependent nature of all things, you become freer and more stable every day. Gradually, you will be in a paradise where the deep love described by the Buddha pervades.

Happiness is not an individual matter; it has the nature of inter being. When you are able to make one friend smile, her happiness will nourish you also. When you find ways to peace, joy and happiness, you do it for everyone. Begin by nourishing yourself with joyful feelings. Practise walking and meditation outside, enjoying the fresh air, the trees, the stars in the night sky. What do you do to nourish yourself? It is important to discuss this subject with dear friends to find concrete ways to nourish joy and happiness.

When you succeed in doing this, your suffering, sorrow and painful mental formations will begin to transform. When your body is invaded by harmful bacteria, your own antibodies surround the bacteria and render them harmless. When there aren't enough antibodies, your body will create more so. It can neutralise the infection. Likewise, when you suffuse your body and mind with feelings of the joy of meditation, your body and spirit will be strengthened. Joyous feelings have a capacity to transform the feelings of sorrow and pain in us.

The Buddha's teachings on love are clear. It is possible to live 24 hours a day in a state of love. The Four Immeasurable Minds are strong concentrations of love, compassion, joy and equanimity. When you dwell in these concentrations, you are living in the most beautiful, peaceful and joyous realm in the universe.

Transform your mind to remain happy

It is precisely the pursuit of happiness which prevents happiness from happening and until this realisation happens, the pursuit must go on.

What is seeking happiness is *Consciousness.* Impersonal consciousness had identified itself with a particular body-mind-organism (form) and a name as a separate entity; and it is this trapped, unidentified consciousness which is seeking its personality. When the ego, the practical seeker of everything in life, takes over the search for happiness, pleasure is mistaken for happiness in the flow of life...The few egos that focus on real happiness become spiritual seekers, for they realise that what they are seeking is not to be found in the flow of life, but in their attitude.

The Greek word, *metanoesis* implies changing the mind, but means transformation of mind. The Sanskrit word for it is *paravritti*, meaning turning around at the deepest level of the heart-mind.

Paravritti tells the seeker-ego that happiness is one's natural state, hidden by hatred born of our perception of the 'other' as a source of potential rivalry and enmity. We are instructed from childhood that *life means competition with the other, and happiness means success over the other,* in the classroom as well as playing fields. The other is seen as a potential enemy.

Whether or not we achieve happiness is based on our sense of personal doership. Buddha said: Events happen, deeds get done, consequences happen, but there is no individual doer of any deed. Everything in life is happening according to the Cosmic Law.

What the sense of personal doership has done is that the human being, at any moment is burdened with an enormous load of hatred for oneself for harming others, willingly or otherwise, and also for the others who hurt us. The total acceptance of personal non-doership means the immediate removal of this load of hatred, and the absence of hatred automatically means the pre-sense of our natural state: happiness, consisting of total peace and harmony.

The Sanskrit term, Sat-Chit-Ananda means *Existence-*

Consciousness-Ananda. Ananda is shanti or peace, not joy or ecstasy. The Buddha said that enlightenment means the end of suffering. It is interesting that the Buddha has used the negative perspective – end of suffering – rather than the positive one of joy or ecstasy. It is the experience of all of us, sometime or the other, that the sudden end of an intense pain has brought about an intensity of relief that was much more acceptable than any positive pleasure or joy. Pursuit of happiness is the very essence of living for all creatures on earth, beginning with the infant seeking its mother's breast. For the poor, happiness can only mean sufficient money to provide the minimum of food, clothing and shelter.

But for those who are reasonably comfortable in life, it is the destiny of a few to look for their happiness beyond what the flow of life could bring. In the case of the unselfish and generous, being generous gives them the happiness they seek, and not being generous would make them unhappy.

Ultimately, happiness means not something in the flow of life, it is the attitude to life. And the most important point about it is that there is no "doing" in it. It is a pure happening.

Pathways to peace and happiness

Our God given abilities are a treasure that is meant for ourselves as well as for the entire world. This wealth should never be misused and made into a burden for us and for others. The greatest tragedy in life is not death; it is to let our great potential, talents, and capabilities go underutilised. When we use the wealth obtained from nature, it diminishes; but when we use the wealth of our inner gifts, it increases.

Today, we search outwardly for the causes and solutions to all the problems of the world. In our haste, we forget the greatest truth of all–that the source of all problems is to be found within the human mind. We forget that the world can become good only if the mind of the individual becomes good. So, along with an understanding of the outer world, it is essential that we also get to know the inner world.

Love is our true essence. Love has no limitations such as religion, race, nationality, or caste. We are all beads strung together on the same thread of love. To awaken this unity and to spread the love that is our inherent nature to others – this is the true aim of human life.

Indeed, love is the only religion that can help humanity rise to great and glorious heights. And love should be the one thread on which all religions and philosophies are strung together. *The beauty of the society lies in the unity of hearts.*

Communication through machines has made people in distant places seem very close. Yet, because of the lack of communication of our hearts, even those who are physically close to us can seem very far away.

Religion and spirituality are the keys with which we can open our hearts and see everyone with compassion. But our minds, being blinded by selfishness, have lost proper judgement; our vision has become distorted. And this attitude will only serve to create more darkness. Using that very same key that is meant to open our hearts, our indiscriminate mindset locks our hearts shut instead.

In today's world, people experience two types of poverty; the poverty caused by lack of food, clothing, and shelter, and the poverty caused by lack of love and compassion. Of these two, the second type needs to be considered first – because, it we have love and compassion in our hearts, then we will wholeheartedly serve those who suffer from lack of food, clothing and shelter.

In order to protect this world, we have to choose a path by which we forsake our personal differences and desires. By forgiving and forgetting, we can try to recreate and give new life to this world. It is useless to dig up and scrutinise the past; it won't benefit anyone. We need to abandon the path of vengeance and retaliation, and impartially evaluate the present world. Only then can we discover the path to true progress.

The body will perish whether we work or sit idle. So instead of rusting away without doing anything for society, it is better to wear oneself out in the pursuit of good actions. Today's world needs people who express goodness in the their words and deeds. If such noble role models can set an example for their fellow beings, the darkness now prevailing in the society will be dispelled, and the light of peace and non-violence will once again illuminate this earth. So, let us work together towards this goal.

Let us grow and unfold as one family, united in love so that we may rejoice and celebrate our oneness in a world where peace and contentment prevail.

Peace feeds happiness

What has peace got to do with happiness? The connections is like that between life and living. For, peace makes life worth living, and paves the way to happiness. Peace and happiness are linked so inextricably that there is no happiness without peace.

What comes first: peace or happiness? Could you be at peace if you are not happy? The answer to these questions depends on your idea of happiness...on whether you get happiness from external factors or from within.

In the Bhagavad Gita, Krishna tells Arjuna that no man can know happiness without peace. However, to experience peace, we need to prepare ourselves to receive it; so in a way, we are responsible for making peace and happiness happen. For peace and happiness to last, both ought to spring from within, regardless of any turmoil or otherwise that is happening outside. The more you internalise your feelings of peace and happiness, the more the chances are of your reaching blissful heights. Once you are able to source peace and happiness from within, you can transcend external vicissitudes to remain ever-happy and blissful.

Reverend Ernest A Fitzgerald described happiness as a 'deep sense of inner peace' that comes when you believe that you are 'making a difference for good in the world'. Thomas Jefferson, former US President, said that 'it is neither wealth nor splendour, but tranquillity and occupation, that give happiness."

From a Buddhist perspective, too, one can learn that 'people inflict pain on others in the selfish pursuit of their happiness or satisfaction. Yet, true happiness comes from a sense of peace and contentment, which in turn must be achieved through the cultivation of altruism, of love and compassion, and elimination of ignorance, selfishness, and greed," in the words of the Dalai Lama. The Buddha said that to "enjoy good health, to bring true happiness to one's family, to bring peace to all, one must first discipline and control one's own mind."

Peace is a recurring prayer in Holy Mass celebrated Christians. The priest chants, 'Peace be with you' and the congregation replies, 'with you also'. The congregation offers each other 'The Sign of Peace'. The mass ends with a blessing by the priest, 'Go in peace, the Mass is ended'.

What, then happens to the non-believer? Is he doomed to turmoil and unhappiness? It would be presumptuous and uncharitable to draw such a conclusion. For, there is peace in the smile of a child; there is peace in the tender touch of one's mother... it has got nothing to do with God or religion, but everything to do with the state of your mind.

Thich Nihat Hanh, the Vietnamese Buddhist monk says that "If in our daily life we can smile, if we can be peaceful and happy, not only we, but everyone will profit from it. This is the most basic kind of peace work." Again, no religious strings are attached to peace.

The Vedic idea of peace includes peace in all areas of life – psychological, social and environmental, for instance. The *Yajur Veda* declares: "Let there be peace in heaven, Let there be peace in the atmosphere, Let there be Peace on Earth…May the waters and medical herbs bring peace, May the trees give peace to all beings, May all the Gods be peaceful, May the Vedas spread peace everywhere, May all other objects everywhere give us peace, And may that peace come to us and remain with us for ever."

Could there be a more sublime yet secular declaration of peace and happiness?

Receipt, Reaction and Response

When we contact the world, three distinct transactions take place: *Receipt of stimuli from the world, reaction within your personality and response to the world.*

Stimuli from the world reach you through your organs of perception. Colour and form enter through your eyes, sound through ears, smell through nose, taste through tongue and touch through skin. Having entered therein, the stimuli react with your mind and intellect. The type of reaction that will set in will depend upon the type of stimulus contacted and the nature of the mind and intellect reacting with it. Consequent to the reaction, your mind and intellect sent out responses back into the world through your organs of action.

Take, for example, your present experience of reading this. *Your eyes are taking in the stimuli in the form of letters and words.* These stimuli reach your mind and intellect. A reaction sets in. It generates a particular type of feeling and judgement depending upon the quality and texture of your mind and intellect. To some, what is generated maybe favourable and they will respond positively, continuing the study. To others, the reaction maybe unfavourable; they will respond negatively and discontinue the study.

The three transactions – receipt, reaction and response – are constantly taking place. The human system resembles the working of a factory. In a manufacturing process also, there are three main operations. Raw material is fed into the factory at one end. The material is processed by machines. The manufactured products are drawn out and despatched at the other end. For best results, all three operations have to be perfected. Raw materials must be of good quality. Machines must be tuned up and operated properly. End products must be tested to meet the requirement standards. So also the three transactions of life have to be regulated properly to ensure a blissful existence.

You are aware that your sense organs constantly perceive sense objects. All sorts of stimuli reach your personality. Check their quality. Avoid inflow of impure and unhealthy stimuli; they create mental agitations. Examine the type of sights that your eyes see, the food that your tongue tastes...Control and regulate your perceptions to ensure the inflow of pure and healthy stimuli.

You must next examine the reactions taking place in you. You may regulate and receive healthy stimuli and yet they may produce unhealthy reactions like jealousy, greed and lust. These reactions are inevitable as they depend upon the nature of your existing mind and intellect. There are two ways of controlling the reactions. The initial and temporary way is to become aware of them and check their effects from spreading further. A permanent control is achieved by rehabilitating your mind and intellect.

The third transaction is the response transmitted by your mind and intellect through the organs of action. Examine the quality of actions perpetrated by your body. If the actions are selfish and self-centred, they tell upon your life. They agitate your mind; they make you unhappy. To avoid this, your actions have to be unselfish. You will experience peace and happiness.

Wherever and whatever you are, perfect these three transactions. No two individuals fit the same description. We are a heterogeneous mixture of personalities. Every individual's nature is best suited for its own evolution.

Chapter - 9

Always Think Positively and Have Happy Thoughts

Power of our positive thoughts

To make our life a meaningful one, we need to mind our thoughts, for our thoughts are the foundation, the inspiration, the motivation power of our deeds. We create our entire world by the way we think. Thoughts are the causes and conditions are the effects.

Our circumstances and conditions are not dictated by the world outside; it is the world inside us that creates the outside. Self-awareness comes from the mind which means soul. Mind is the sum total of the states of consciousness grouped under thought, will and feeling. Besides self-consciousness, we have the power to choose and think. Krishna says: "No man resteth a moment inactive". Even when inactive on the bodily plane, we are all the time acting on the thought plane. Therefore, if we observe ourselves, we can easily mould our thoughts. If our thoughts are pure and noble, naturally actions follow the same. If our thoughts are filled with jealousy, hatred and greed, our actions will be the same.

Trying to keep thoughts from our minds can produce the very state we are trying to avoid. We can alter our environment to create the mood. When, for instance, we are depressed, if we sit by ourselves trying to think cheerful thoughts, we often do not succeed. But if we mix with people who are cheerful, we can bring about a change in our mood and thoughts. Every thought we think, every act we perform, creates in us an impression, and that impression, like everything else, is subject to cyclic law and becomes repetitive in our mind. So we alone have the choice to create our thoughts and develop the kind of impressions that make our action more positive.

If there are two piles, one of gold and one of dirt, which one will you choose? The gold one. If there is only one pile in which the dirt and gold are mixed, you would try to separate the gold from the dirt and take the gold. We need to do the same with our personality.

We tend to overlook the good things, preferring instead, to focus on all that's bad. So despite having so much to give, so much to receive and so many positive qualities within, we end up identifying ourselves with the negative. We can help ourselves to separate the negative from the positive; to select and hold on to the positive. It we want to overcome likes and dislikes, desires and rejections, we have to learn to bring out and appreciate the positivity of life. That positivity has to be expressed in every situation, whether it is an exam, a human relationship, social living or reclusive living.

You go through various experiences, some good, some bad. Whenever you react, it is a bad experience and whenever you accept and act, it is a positive experience. This positivity and acceptance has to be focus in life if you want to succeed. This is real Yoga. If this focus is lost, then do not claim to be a practitioner of Yoga. You can only claim to be a practitioner of Asana, or only a physical part of Yoga-meditation.

Change has to come from within. Harmony should be experienced both externally and internally. If you identify only with the inner experience, with the inner state of happiness, and there is reaction in external attitudes, behaviour, relationship and communication, then that experience can never be complete.

Author Tom Peters, an expert on management skills, has examined well-run corporations for years to discover the secrets of their excellence. Much of what he found can be applied to personal relationships. One key to corporate excellence is a minimum of conflict. Companies that have defused corporate discord know it's importance not to focus on problems. Instead of zeroing in on what someone did wrong, they pay attention to the things people do well.

Similarly, how a couple looks at their marriage can make all the difference between having a relationship that centres on problems and arguments, and one that encourages respect and love.

Let us choose the thought seeds of right ideas, noble and courageous aspirations that will be received by minds of the same nature. Right introspection will be required of us to determine what we really desire to effect. Everything in the universe is inter-related and interdependent, that we live in with one another and by accepting the grand principle of universal brotherhood, we shall be in a position to appreciate what a heavy responsibility is ours to think right. Let us reflect and send loving and helpful thoughts and lighten the load of world's suffering.

Cope with negative attitude

Another thing that we need to change is our negative attitude to life. So few seem to be truly happy. Happiness is relative. It has little to do with money, fame or power: Why else do so many people who have all three end up leading miserable lives? A positive attitude will make you grow. You will be able to achieve happiness and spread it around, making the world a better place to live in.

A cat before a mirror doesn't know it's looking at its own reflection. It thinks there is another cat in front of her. But a baby by the age of two realises she is seeing her own image in a mirror. This self-awareness, unique to humans, makes us compare our happiness levels with those of people we know well, like friends, relatives, or colleagues. We are constantly bothered that other people are perhaps living more fulfilled lives.

One practical way to become happier is by reading up on the huge number of happiness surveys done worldwide. When you learn how millions of diverse humans think and feel about their lives, you get perspective on your own. You become less prone to irrational negative thoughts. It's good to learn that it's human nature to be dissatisfied. Someone else's dish at a restaurant looks more appetising that what you have ordered. Buy three out of eight shirts you like and you fret later about not choosing the others. Holiday anywhere and you wonder if you should have gone elsewhere. This nagging self-doubt lessens when you remember that being dissatisfied is a part of the human condition. Once we understand this, we can cope better with our own dissatisfaction.

Talking of money most people think they'd become very happy if they got lots of it. This doesn't happen in real life. Money apart, many people suffer from a sense of being wronged. Whether at the workplace or within a family, most individuals imagine they don't get their due. This persecution mania in varying degrees is also part of the human condition. Our aggrieved condition usually has little basis. We may think somebody wants to hurt us, but that person isn't even thinking of us, so immersed is he in his own life. The "persecuted" man doesn't know this, and he may spend his whole life nursing grievances. Allied to a persecution mania is a common feeling that while you struggle, many people enjoy undeserved success. They do, but they are outnumbered a hundred to one by deserving successful people. In life, merit counts far more than incompetence.

We all know that if water stands still for some days, it starts to smell foul. It remains fresh and clean only when it flows. The same is the case with our emotions. For a healthy emotional status, emotions must flow continuously. Basically, there are two ways to handle our emotions. Our solid emotional system or hard wired emotions see to it that a particular emotion once fed into our brain remains there solidified for ever.

For example, if a person does something bad to us, we store that bad taste or emotion in our memory permanently. We thus create a permanent bad impression in us about that person. This stored negative emotion and many such others, radiates negative energy that ultimately distorts our personality in a negative way. But there is a better way to handle the same situation. It means trying to forget the bad things done unto us as early as possible. It's best not to store any emotion permanently in a 'file'. We must learn to delete bad memory files.

Take the example of the flowing river. If there is a big rock in the riverbed, the river simply flows around it and carries on with its journey. The river does not come into conflict with the immovable object. Similarly, personal attainment is only a selfish subjective attainment. That attainment can be lost at any time. It is easy to attain and also easy to lose because life follows a *principle of give and take.* That is the flow of life with which yoga identifies.

In the beginning yoga is a practice, then it becomes a way of life. When it becomes a way of life, identification with an expression of the balanced, positive and optimistic nature takes place and then one attains physical, mental and spiritual wealth.

Since everybody seeks happiness, millions of people try to find it through religion. Most discourses, however, tend to focus more on scriptures and topics like reincarnation. They don't provide much graphic insight into people's daily mental state. But scientific study and research attempt to do so. Take any emotion from happiness, sadness to shame or envy and they have been studied thoroughly. Remember that human beings are unequal, even within a family. Who's heard of Bill Gate's relatives or Sachin Tendulkar's? You will always have a few relatives, friends, ex-classmates, or colleagues who are smarter, richer, or better-looking than you. Envying them will burn you inside. Bertrand Russell said that the most enviable man is the man who feels no envy.

Positive thinking and a positive attitude may indeed have

power. That belief has long been a conjecture, but in recent years, scientists studying the mind-body connections and interactions are finding that an optimistic outlook can improve more than just mental health.

There is a science that is emerging that says a positive attitude isn't just a state of mind. It also has linkages to what is going on in the brain and in the body. Science in this area is at the very beginning. Although clearly defined scales, such as those used for measuring depression, don't exist for studying happiness, scientific recognition of a mind-body connection is gathering steam.

Hone in something beyond the illness and dedicating oneself to cures for the illness rather than dwelling on one's illness gives purpose to life, and helps prevent the negative effects of stress while medical science does its work. People need to think not in terms of a cure, but of a better life.

It's putting an impossible burden on the power of positive thinking to say that people should be cured. The right way to think is that this positive orientation can actually keep life worth living and can possibly extend the period of life you have.

Young are agents of positive change

The period of youth is pivotal for human development. A critical period of personal change, this is when you begin to consciously explore and apply your knowledge, values and beliefs about individual and collective life. You take on new responsibilities, becoming agents of change in your communities. Young, you are not victims in need of others to solve your problems. Rather, your age group represents a tremendous source of intellectual and social potential waiting to be developed and channelled towards socially constructive ends.

The future will depend a great deal on the manner in which educational programmes and methods are designed to release your latent potential, preparing you for the world you are to inherit. The connection between education and individual and collective well beings is well established and it is imperative to focus on a particular dimension of education, namely education in service of community, which, in our experience, is central to the transformation of individual and community life.

Forces that influence the intellectual and emotional development of a child are not confined to the classroom. Media, technology, family, peers, the wider community and other social institutions covey messages that maybe reinforcing in some respects and contradictory in others, which could add to your confusion – about identity, moral purpose and social reality. As such, formal education needs to go beyond the exclusive aim of helping you to secure gainful employment. Educational processes need to assist you to recognise and express your potential while developing in you the capacity to contribute to the spiritual and material prosperity of communities.

The concept of a twofold moral purpose – to develop your inherent potential and to contribute to a transformation of society – provides an important axis of the educational process. Many educational programmes perceive young people as mere receptacles of information. To challenge these trends, the Bahai community endeavours a develop culture which promotes an independent way of thinking, studying and acting, in which students see themselves as united by a desire to work for common good, supporting one another and advancing together, respectful each one's knowledge.

Knowledge is the key if you wish to flourish. Access to knowledge is the right of every human being. The responsibility to generate new knowledge and apply it in socially beneficial ways rests on your shoulders. In the same way, the creation of an environment conducive to this process is a duty of every government. Without access to knowledge, your meaningful participation in community affairs is not possible. The primary focus of educational processes, then, must be to build capacity in young people like you to participate fully as protagonists of social progress.

Inequities of girls' access to quality education must be addressed for this would have a 'multiplier effect' – it results in reduced chances of early marriage, greater likelihood of their informed and active role in family planning, reduced infant and maternal mortality, enhanced participation in social, economic and political decision-making and promotion of economic prosperity. The equality of men and women, boys and girls is a fundamental truth about human reality and not just a desirable condition to be achieved for the good of the society.

Positive thoughts and feelings may help your ticker thrive

Depression, social isolation, anxiety, hostility, emotional stress etc., when it comes to heart disease, the negative aspects of psychological functioning have gotten most of the attention. They have been shown to increase the chances of developing various sorts of cardiovascular diseases, and they can made existing conditions worse. What about the flip side? Can happiness or an upbeat approach to life protect the heart and blood vessels? Folk wisdom says yes. But there is precious little hard data to back up this notion. A small number of studies have demonstrated that positive thoughts or an optimistic outlook confer some protection. The latest contribution in this area looks at positive feelings.

Psychologists Laura Kubzansky of the Harvard School of Public Health and Rebecca Thurston of the University of Pittsburgh School of Medicine studied the impact of emotional vitality. This gauges a person's feelings of energy, sense of well-beings, and ability to regulate his or her emotions.

The researchers crunched information collected between 1971 and 1975 from more than 6,000 initially healthy men and women taking part in America's first National Health and Nutrition Examination Survey. Based on answers to six questions (see "Rating Emotional Vitality"), they classified each participant as having low, moderate, or high emotional vitality.

During the 15-year period following the health survey, far fewer people in high emotional vitality group had a heart attack, developed angina or another form of coronary artery disease, or died of heart disease, compared with individuals in the low vitality group. The difference amounted to as much as three per cent, which could translate into thousands of fewer cases of heart diseases or deaths each year.

Greater emotional vitality was not just a stand-in for less depression – its benefits remained after the researchers took depression into account. Instead, it seemed to exert its own special effect.

How could feeling energetic, having a sense of well-being, or being on an even emotional keel guard the heart? By counteracting stress, emotional vitality could calm the stress-induced arousal of the nervous system that boosts heart rate, elevates blood pressure, and activates inflammation and other heart disease-promoting processes. Positive emotions might contribute to an individual's sense of control over his or her destiny, which has been associated with protection against heart disease. It might make it easier to make or use social connections. Then again, it could be that people with high emotional vitality are less likely to develop heart disease because they have healthier behaviour and habits, like smoking less, exercising more, or controlling their weight.

Half-glass-full attitude

Your genes, early learning, and family and social environments set the stage for whether your outlook on life is essentially positive or negative. If yours is a bit on the negative side, don't despair. It isn't set in stone (or the legion of psychiatrists, psychologists, and other mental health counsellors would be searching for work!) and working to improve it is actually one of the hottest trends in mental health. This goes beyond the "power of positive thinking." It involves several different approaches. Here are a few.

- **Deliberately focus** on events (e.g. a holiday in Shimla) or activities (a cool swim on a hot Saturday afternoon) that give you pleasure and take a mental snapshot to recall later.
- **Maintain a "gratitude journal"** where you can jot down the things that you enjoyed doing, so you can relive those events/activities every time you read it, or share the experiences with others.
- **Engage in activities that call on your inherent strengths** either at work, home or play. For instance, if you have talent for managing people, and you are stuck in Accounts, ask for a transfer to HRD.
- **Apply your strengths to something outside yourself** that helps you create meaning in your life. It could be religion, nature, art, volunteering, or something else.

Do not let go of the child in you

What are we doing on this Earth? I asked. "Honestly? I don't know. I have looked for answers in many corners, in illuminated and in dark places; today I am convinced that no one knows – only God does," he replied.

"That isn't a good answer from a Master", I said.

It is an honest answer. I know many people who will explain the reason for our existence in details. Don't believe them as these people are still imprisoned in the old language and they only believe in things that have explanation," I replied.

"Does it mean that there isn't a reason for living?"

"You didn't understand what I said. I said I don't know the

reason. But of course there is a reason for us to be here and God knows it."

"Why isn't it revealed to us?" I continued.

"It is revealed to each one of us, but in a language that sometimes we don't accept because it isn't logical – and we are far too used to recipes and formulas. Our hearts know why we are here. Those who are listening to their hearts follow the signs and live their personal legends will understand that they are taking part in something even if they don't comprehend it rationally. The tradition says that in the second before our death, we realise the true reason of existence. And at this moment, Hell and Paradise are born.

"I don't understand that."

"Hell is, in this precise moment, to look back and know we have wasted an opportunity to honour God and dignify life's miracle. Paradise is to be able to say, at this moment, 'I have made some mistakes, but I wasn't a coward. I lived my life and did what I had to do.' Hell and Paradise will follow us for a long time but not forever."

"How can I tell if I am living the life I am supposed to live?"

"If you experience enthusiasm, instead of bitterness. That is the only difference. As for the rest, we ought to respect mystery and accept – with humbleness – that God has a plan for us. A generous plan, which conducts us towards His presence and which justifies these millions of stars, planets and blackholes that we are seeing this evening, here in Oslo." (We were in Norway at the time). "It is very hard to live without an explanation."

"Can you explain why people need to give and receive love? No. And you live with that, don't you? You not only live with that, but it is also the most important thing in life: Love. And there is no explanation."

"It is the same regarding the explanation for life, there is no explanation. But there is a reason for us to be here, and you need to be humble enough to accept that. Trust my words, each human being's life has a meaning even though we make the mistake of spending a great part of our lives on Earth seeking an answer, while we forget to live."

He continued, "I can give you an example from a time where I got close to understanding all that. I was at my 50-year high school commemoration party. There, at the school where I studied when I was a teenage, I found many friends. We drank, we told the same jokes we had at heart half a century before. At a certain moment, I looked out to the schoolyard. Then, I saw myself as a child, playing with my friends, looking at life with surprise and intensity. Suddenly that child I had been seemed to gain force and began to approach me. It looked me in the eyes and smiled. Then I understood that I hadn't betrayed my childhood dreams, that the child I had been one day was still proud of me; that the same reason I had to live as a child stayed alive in my heart."

"Seek to live with the same intensity as you did when you were a child. The child doesn't ask for explanations; he dives into each day as if it were a different adventure, and at night, he sleeps tired and happy."

Positively positive!

You are what you think. You feel what you want. Do you frequently hear yourself saying or thinking, 'I cant', If you say this often enough, you will soon believe it. It will become a self-fulfilling prophecy and you will feel more powerless and out of control. Adopt the turnaround mentality: Believe in yourself and realise that you are a capable person. Give yourself positive, encouraging statements. If your goal requires a response or approval from others, you revert to feeling helpless and feel out of control. Work at feeling good about yourself and become more self-reliant. Seek help when you need it.

Scientists have come up with proof of the power of positive thinking. Positive thinkers live longer than those who are constantly worrying. Positive self-perceptions can also prolong life expectancy, say Yale University researchers. The research suggests that people who feel bad about getting old accelerate the ageing process. A positive attitude will add more years to your life that not smoking or taking regular exercise.

All of our feelings, beliefs and knowledge are based on our internal thoughts, both conscious and subconscious. We are in control, whether we know it or not.

Think a happy thought

Your thoughts have a direct influence on the way you feel and behave. If you tend to dwell on sad or negative thoughts, you most likely are not a very happy person. Likewise, if you think that your job is enough to give you a headache, you probably will come home with throbbing temples each day. This is just another clear example of the power the mind exerts over the body.

Your imagination can be a powerful tool to help you combat stress, tension and anxiety. You can use visualisation to harness the energy of your imagination, and it does not take long-probably just a few weeks to master the technique. Try to visualise two or three times a day. Most people find it easiest to do in bed in the morning and at night before falling asleep, though with practice you'll be able to visualise whenever and wherever the need arises. To begin visualisation, sit or kneel down in a comfortable position and close your eyes. Scan your body for any muscle tension and relax the areas that need it.

Once you feel relaxed, begin to visualise a scene, object, or place that is soothing and pleasing to you. Imagine every aspect of the scene, involving all of your senses. For example, if you like to visualise a waterfall on a mountain, imagine first what this looks like: the rushing water, the stream flowing from it, the size and thickness of the trees all around.

Another type of visualisation involves an image that you associate with tension which you can replace with an image for relaxation. For example, you might visualise tension as a taut rope, the sound of thunder, the coloured, pitch darkness, persistent hammering, or blinding white light. These images of tension can so often fade into images of relaxation.

For instance, the taut rope loosens, the thunder subsides and is replaced by a light rain, red turns to orchid, the darkness begins to lighten, the pounding hammer is replaced by the murmur of cicadas and crickets, the blinding white light softens to a sunset. As you become more involved in your visual image, your body will relax and you will be able to let go of the problems or worries that you'd felt before.

Chapter - 10

Laughter/Humour is God's Gift for Happiness

Wit and wisdom are inextricably connected. The wise man is who is most carefree who takes whatever comes his way with understanding and good humour. Even the ordinary man knows that laughter is the best medicine. You should also discover how to laugh at yourself and this crazy world we live in. The ability to laugh freely and frequently at humorous events is healthy and desirable. It is not a gift of mind it is a gift of heart.

When you begin your day in laughter and love, your life gets divinely enlivened. True prayer is laughing in the morning both from outside and from deep inside. Shri Ravishankar states that laughter comes from the centre of our Being, from the core of our heart. Our belly is so full of laughter that the laughter permeates every cell in our body. *True laughter is true prayer.* When you laugh, the whole of nature laughs with you. It echoes and resounds and makes life worthwhile. When things go all right, everybody can laugh, but when everything falls apart, and yet you laugh, that is evolution and growth. Nothing in life is more worthy than your laughter. Never lose it. Events come and go. Some are pleasant, and others, unpleasant. There is some area deep in you that is left untouched. Hold on to what is untouched. Then you will be able to keep laughing.

Sometimes you laugh just to avoid thinking or to avoid looking at yourself. But when you see and feel within that life is present and intense every moment, nothing can bother you or touch you. That laughter is authentic. You might have observed babies, six months or one year old. When they laugh, their whole body is jumping and bouncing. Every cell in the body is laughing. That is enlightenment. That laughter is innocent, pure, without inhibitions.

When life's essence blooms from within, that is true laughter akin to Godliness. Godliness is a feeling of belonging. We all belong to one another. Laughter opens us up, opens the heart. And anytime we don't feel up to that innocence, what do we do? "We feel tense, we don't feel that innocent or free."

Smiling is one of the most effective means of dissolving

anxiety, anger and over-reaction. If you ensure that you keep a half smile on your face, even in the most difficult situation, you will be able to deal with unpleasant feelings, in a far more rational and empowered manner. A constant smile reinforces that state of tranquillity and joyfulness, which is the most critical foundation for holistic health. It subconsciously also emphasises, that every moment can be pleasant in your life. It has also been scientifically discovered that smiling and laughing release chemicals in your body that combat stress and disease. Not surprisingly, most Yoga sessions include this in their regime. Hence, we must encourage all those in our circle of influence to smile more often and to be free of anxiety.

Humour many be one of the most effective means of avoiding or derailing an argument. The story told to me goes like this. One of his friends was arguing with his wife, early in their marriage. "It reached the heights of absurdity." Finally, he said quite seriously, 'You know what they would do to you in Russia if you did this? They'd take you out before a firing squad! "What she said in response to was, 'So I made a little mistake-shoot me!' He started laughing at this reply. After he stopped laughing, her words made him realise how absurd the argument had become."

Once Martin Luther had said that if he is not allowed to laugh in heaven, he would not want to go there. If a man insisted always on being serious, and never allowed himself a bit of fun and relaxation, he would go mad or become crazy. Nothing in life is more worthy than your laughter. Never lose it. Events come and go. Some are pleasant and others unpleasant. There is some area deep in you that is left untouched. Hold on to what is untouched. Then you will be able to keep laughing.

It is like putting a key in a car ignition point which the engine catches and turns it over. Your diaphragms interprets as a real one and a genuine laughter follows. You should also make time for laughter and can use humour with customers, if you are a salesman. *Laughter is the shortest distance between two people.* Through humour, you can soften the worst that life delivers, says comedian, Bill Casley. Once you find laugher, no matter how painful your situation be, you can survive it. Laughter is a skill we can all acquire because it comes naturally. But it is also something that can be nurtured.

Lastly, I am happy to say that the Osho World celebrates 'World Laughing Day' and I repeat below some thoughts about it as expressed by Osho:

"Their whole play of existence is so beautiful that laughter can be the only response to it."

Laughter is far more sacred than prayer, because prayer can be done by anyone, whereas to laugh, one needs to have presence of mind; a quickness of seeing into things.

Never go towards God seriously; go laughing and dancing, and your prayer will be heard...and your thank-you will reach the address. The deeper your laughter; the deeper will become your prayer. If you can dance, you have entered the shrine, you have come close to God. I am releasing a sense of humour in you, a deep laughter in you. Laughter is prayer, it is more spiritual than chanting *mantras*, it is far more cosmic than going to a place of worship. Let your laughter be your only prayer. Let your joy be your only offering. Love life! Love small things! Don't miss a single moment.

Laughter has tremendous beauty, a lightness. It will bring lightness to you, and it will give you wings to fly. A good laugh is tremendously meditative. Laughter is not irreligious. Laughter is one of the most evolved phenomena in human life. No other animal can laugh, it is only man who can laugh.

Dr. Raymond Moody, Jr, who wrote the book-*Laugh After Laugh: The Healing Power of Humour*-states that his sense of humour helped him getting through the terrible grind of medical college. He states that he came to feel that a human being's ability to laugh is just as valid an indicator of health as are all those other things that doctors check. Gradually, many members of the medical establishment are coming around to that thinking. A study on the beneficial effects of laughter shows that when we laugh, muscles are activated. When we stop laughing, these muscles relax and as such, some painful conditions of the body benefit greatly from the dose of laughter.

In India, the Sony T.V. channel has started giving programmes on laughter-*The Great Indian Laughter Champions* which has become most popular and successful programme and which nobody wants to miss it.

How can we all get more laughter into our lives? Mix with people who laugh because their joy rubs off on those around them. *Practise the art of laughing*. Even fake laughter triggers the diaphragm.

Laughter heals you and it really is the best medicine

It promotes healing by speeding up your blood flow. It's no joke being stuck in a hospital bed. But it seems that the old adage is: *True laughter really is the best medicine. It is likely to put you* on the road to recovery more quickly than any hi-tech treatment, simply by increasing your circulation, researchers have found.

A five-year study of patients with leg ulcers has established that a hearty chuckle stimulates the diaphragm which in turn, plays a vital role in moving blood around the body. It actually speeds recovery from leg ulcers, said the report by the University of *Leeds' School of Healthcare.*

In contrast, expensive ultrasound therapy does little to help, contrary to what the researchers had expected to find. Traditional nursing care is also effective and this human contact is likely to lead to jokes and banter which is where the laughter therapy comes in. The research, published by the British Medical Journal, said: "Forget technology. The best prescription for patients with venous leg ulcers is good quality nursing care and the occasional belly laugh!" About 500,000 people suffer from recurrent leg ulcers in the UK. They are common in those with varicose veins or mobility problems and the condition is becoming more common with increased obesity. The older and larger ulcers become, the harder they are to get rid of. Hence, the search for solutions that could speed the healing process.

A number of small studies had suggested that ultrasound could be the answer. Professor Andrea Nelson, who led the study, said : "The key to caring for this group of patients is to stimulate blood flow back up the legs to the heart. 'The best way to do that is with compression bandages and support stockings not 'magic wands' – coupled with advice on diet and exercise. "Believe it or not, having a really hearty chuckle can help too. This is because laughing gets the diaphragm moving and this plays a vital part in moving blood around the body." Complicated leg ulcers can take six months or more to heal. *Ultrasound therapy* did not speed this up – but did add an average of Rs.14,574 per patient to their care bill.

Previous studies have shown laughter can ward off heart disease. Loma Linda University in California studied men and women taking medication for diabetes, high blood pressure and high cholesterol. Those who were prescribed "mirthful laughter" in the form of 30 minutes of comedy every day found their stress hormone levels fell.

Laugher boosts your immunity

Laughter increases the white blood cell activity and boosts the immune system, says a study done by Stanford University. It improves one's health and helps a person with terminal illness like cancer heal faster. Research also shows that it lowers blood pressure, reduces stress hormones and makes you feel much lighter. It induces certain biological changes in the body, which do the magic. "Laughter boosts levels of endorphins, the body's natural painkillers and suppresses the stress hormones. It also increases the cells that destroy viruses and tumours," says yoga trainer, Zayed Khan. A good laugh exercises your lungs and circulatory system and increases the amount of oxygen in your blood. That makes watching those comedy shows a healthy activity too. No doubt, cracking up is the best stress buster.

Doctors, too, have a sense of humour

One normally thinks of medicine as an entirely serious business but it has its lighter moments. *Sir Arthur Conan Doyle, the creator of Sherlock Holmes, had practised medicine before changing over to detective fiction.* There is a story that in one of his earlier income tax returns he had entered his earnings as 200 pounds. The inspector returned the form with 'Most unsatisfactory' prominently scrawled across it. Conan Doyle himself added," I agree" and returned it.

It is not so well-known that 'W.G.' the great cricketer, was also a qualified surgeon. When he retired to practise medicine again, he wrote : "My time spent in cricket will not have been wasted. As a surgeon, I will often be called on to make a good 'cut', while my experience in drawing stump will encourage me to attempt dental surgery. In the game I was generally 'well set'. Reporters may have to say the same of my patients' broken legs and arms now."

Dr. Amherst, who attended Queen Elizabeth I, was asked by her: "What is the time, doctor?" "Whatever it may please your Majesty," came the cautious reply. Not all men of medicine are as cautious in their replies. John Radcliffe served William III. The king, pointing to his swollen legs which were in contrast to the rest of the emaciated body asked:

"What think you of these, doctor?"

"Why truly I would not have these two for your Majesty's three kingdoms."

Sure enough, this was the doctor's last appearance in the court.

The story is provided by Sir Frederick Treves, surgeon to Edward VII, who attained fame from the celebrated 'Elephant Man case.' When a distinguished patient complained of the painful nature of his illness, Sir Frederick smilingly replied: "Permit me to congratulate you. You are the lucky possessor of an illness which hitherto has been thought to be extinct."

'Bombastic' is a familiar word. Ever suspected for a moment how it came to be coined? Theophrastus Bombastus Von Hohenheim, the great Swiss-born doctor, bequeathed the word to posterity by his behaviour. He delighted in burning well-known medical books – including the works of Galen and Avicenna – before his students at the University of Basel, insisted always: "You will not need them. Patients are the only books. Not even a dog-killer can learn his trade from books."

Sometimes an alert patient may occasionally give considerable embarrassment. But not if the doctor has the presence of mind of Sir Richard Jebb at Cambridge for many years.

"Pray Sir, may I eat pork?" asked a lady patient.

"Why, it's the best thing you could take."

"I am so glad doctor. But the other day you said it was the worst thing for me."

"The other day, Madam, was Tuesday. This isn't Tuesday, is it?"

Nostradamus practised not only prophecy and astrology but medicine as well. Having fallen from grace, he faced an almost certain prospect of being put to death. Sardonically, Charles IX (France) asked him whether he could foretell the hour of his death.

"Sir," said Nostradamus, 'Fate has withheld the exact hour of my death, but the stars have decreed that I die shortly before your Majesty. You will not survive me."

Nostradamus stayed on to be taken by the king as his own astronomer.

Franz Mesmer, founder Mesmerism, often stigmatised for his unconventional prescriptions by the medical faculty, was summoned by Madame Campan to cure her husband of pulmonary inflammation. True to reputation, the doctor advised that the only cure for her husband was to lay in the bed, one of the three things – "a young woman of brown complexion, a black hen or an old bottle." Madame Compan pleased: "Sir, if the choice be a matter of indifference, pray try the empty bottle."

Incidentally, ever suspected that Chekhov, Maugham, Axel

Munthe, Samuel Smiles and Robert Bridges were doctors before attaining literary fame? Pierre Janet, famous French neurologist, once wrote: "If a patient is poor he is committed to a public hospital as a 'psychotic'. If he can afford a sanatorium, the diagnosis is 'neurasthenia'. If he is wealthy enough to be in his own home under constant watch of nurses and physicians he is simply an 'indisposed eccentric!" So much for the differing yardsticks.

After the doctor had finished examining the patient, he advised: "Just stop smoking and drinking. Go to bed early. Get up at the crack of dawn."

Recovering, the patient pleaded: "Surely I don't deserve the best. What is the second best, doctor?"

Well, most of us have also heard the old saying: "if you go to a doctor, you might get cured in a week, otherwise, it takes seven days." Think it over once again!

One life to laugh

It is medicine that probably no doctor in the world will prescribe to you...But it works wonders, spreads joy and enlivens people's lives like a sparkling chandelier. Laughter is a magic drug, use it... Says Osho. For centuries, religion has been a serious affair for most of the believers – it has been too ritualistic and grim. Being holy started getting equated with seriousness. Hence, the so called religion deprived people of their natural innocent laughter.

By performing so many rituals, people became egoistic; the priests and religious followers started feeling holier than others. Others who weren't practising the routine rituals were condemned as unholy. So to avoid being condemned by holy people, ordinary people started conducting religious affairs just out of guilt. Religion became serious and most of the people have been living with that burden on their hearts – they have forgotten to laugh and celebrate.

Osho said:"*Religion cannot be anything other than a celebration of life.* And the serious person becomes handicapped. He creates barriers; he cannot dance or sing... The dimension of celebration disappears from his life. He becomes desert like. And if you are a desert, you can go on thinking and pretending that you are religious but you're not. You maybe sectarian, but not religious."

Osho brought a revolution in the realm of religiousness. He introduced laughter as a cleansing process. During one of his discourses on the *Akshya Upanishad,* he explained the place and significance of laughter in human life. There are three types of laughter...

The first is when you laugh at someone else. This is the meanest, the lowest when you laugh at somebody else's expense. This is aggressive and insulting. Deep down in this laughter, there always is a feeling of revenge.

The second type is when you laugh at yourself. This is worth achieving and cultured.

And this man is valuable who can laugh at himself. He has risen above vulgarity. He has risen above hatred, aggression and violence.

The third is just cosmic. You laugh at the situation as it is. The whole situation, as it is, is absurd – no purpose in the future, no beginning in the beginning. The whole situation of existence is such that if you can see the whole, such a great vastness moving toward no fixed purpose, no goal, laughter will arise. Osho introduced laughter as meditation. This is a five minute morning meditation that one could to first thing in the morning for a cheerful day ahead.

"Every morning upon waking, before opening your eyes, stretch like a cat. Stretch every fibre of your body. After about four minutes, with eyes still closed, start laughing. For five minutes just laugh. At first you will be doing it, but soon the sound of your attempt will cause genuine laughter. Lose yourself in laughter. It may take several days before it really happens, for we are so unaccustomed to the phenomenon. But before long it will be spontaneous and will change the whole nature of your day."

He adds: "My own understanding is that there is nothing more valuable than laughter. Laughter brings you closest to prayer."

Laughter brings you to the earth, brings you down from your stupid ideas of being holier-than-thou. Laughter brings you to reality as it is. The world is a play of God, a cosmic joke. Unless you understand it as a cosmic joke you will never be able to understand the ultimate mystery.

Laughter yoga: the latest mind-body therapy

Laughter yoga, was developed in India by *Dr. Madan Kataria*. In laughter yoga, people are led through their laughing exercises, interspersed with deep breathing. "It's one of the healthiest things that you could do for yourself," says laughter therapy specialist, Dr. Santosh Sahi. Ten minutes of hearty laughter equals 30 minutes on the rowing machine, says research by the Stanford University.

This practice combines laughter sessions with easy aerobic exercises and has many physiological and emotional benefits, thereby making it a unique well-being workout. "The reason we call it laughter yoga is because it combines *laughter exercises with yoga breathing.* This brings more oxygen to the body and the brain which makes one feel more energetic, healthy and stress-free," says Dr. Sahi.

While natural laugh in daily life lasts hardly for minutes, it is not powerful enough to bring about physiological changes. With laughter yoga, one laughs continuously for 15 to 20 minutes with short breaks of yogic breathing. Except for pregnant women, who can face undue pressure in the abdomen by laughing, this therapy works magic for almost anybody. "It allows people with serious illnesses to vent out their unpleasant emotions," she says. Interestingly, laughter yoga was initially started as social club movement but now it has entered the business world too. In fact a one year laughter yoga trial in a Danish IT firm showed that the company's sales increased more than 25 percent and the stress levels came down by 75 percent.

Surround yourself with humour

Laughter elevates mood, promotes creativity and give us energy. According to one study, the average *four-year-old laughs three hundred times a day,* while the average *adult laughs just about fifteen times.* With all the obligations, stresses and activities that fill our days, we have forgotten how to laugh. Daily laughter has been shown to elevate our moods, promote creativity and give us more energy. Comedian Steve Martin reportedly laughs for five minutes in front of the mirror every morning to get his creative juices flowing and to start his day on a high note. Try it; it works.

Laughter therapy has even been used to cure illnesses and heal those with serious ailments. As William James, the father of modern psychology observed, "We don't laugh because we are happy. We are happy because we laugh."

A friend of mine, always known for his wise ways, made it his new year's resolution, one year, to laugh more. Every few weeks, he would go to his local video store and rent a *Three Stooges* movie or buy a new book of humour, which he would then dip into when he had a few free moments during the course of his day.

A positive person already, he began to notice that he felt even happier and started to laugh even more than before he undertook this personal development initiative. Because of all the humour, he surrounded himself with and the new awareness it created in his life, he also began to see the lighter side of things and no longer experienced the level of stress he had felt in his professional pursuits. This simple discipline raised him to a whole new level of living and effectiveness.

Why not follow my friend's lead and head down to your local video store to stock up on the latest funny movies? Then pick up a few books, perhaps something from Gary Larson's *Far Side* series or the much – read *Dilbert* cartoons, to stimulate your laughter habit. Reconnect to your playful side and enjoy the wonders of a deep belly laugh.

The power of smile

It's 7 AM, a mother of two, would love more sleep, but she can hear her five month old son, Angus, rousing the next room. "I am hardly able to drag myself out of bed," says Jenks, who, with both an infant and an older son age two, is no stranger to fatigue. "But when I look into his crib, and he gives me a big smile, it fills me with joy – and then everything is fine."

Such is the power of a simple smile. In fact, research over the last two decades has been proving scientifically what aphorisms and popular song makes the eyes crinkle. Scientists have discovered that a genuine smile is a marker of real happiness. The fake smile – sometimes called the flight attendant smile – uses only the first muscle set and is generally used as a form of courtesy.

In one of his most famous studies, Keltner and colleague Lee Anne Harker coded the smiles of 114 women who posed for their college yearbook photo in 1958 and 1960. All but three smiled, but 61 did the fake courtesy smile. Keltner's study found that over 30 years of follow-up, the women who displayed genuine smiles were more apt to get married and remain married, and scored higher on tests of emotional and physical well-being. Other Keltner studies have found that people who display spontaneous, real smiles are better able to overcome stressful events, such as the death of a spouse, and that couples who show loving smiles when talking about each other release oxytocin – called the caring hormone and associated with bonding and reproduction – into the blood.

Keltner notes that while some people are born with happier temperaments, which set them up for success, others can become happier by being taught how to cultivate a genuine smile. *Smile, and the whole world smiles with you, and grey skies really will clear up if you put on a happy face.*

"A smile is central to our evolution and one of the most powerful tools of human behaviour, "says Dacher Keltner, a professor of psychology at the University of California, who has studied the importance of facial expression – including the variety and impact of smiles.

Anyone who has been around a smiling baby knows how a spontaneous grin helps build kinship, strengthen social bonds and release positive smile. " In the happiness literature," says Keltner, "the greatest association with happiness is connection to others. Teaching smiling is important because it helps us connect."

Putting on a happy face not only helps us make friends, it translates into altered brain chemistry that makes us feel better. Ekman and University of Wisconsin neuroscientist Richard Davidson used brain scans to show that the genuine smile activates some parts of the brain associated with pleasure and happiness, though it does not activate the full pattern associated with these emotions. They found that if people learnt how to activate the muscles of the Duchenne smile, even artificially, they could produce similar brain activity.

Since smiling is so important to happiness and social connection, losing one's smile is devastating. Twice in his adult life Ross Main, who operates a guest house in Canada, has had half his face paralysed by Bell's palsy, a disorder in which the seventh cranial nerve becomes inflamed, probably from a viral infection. "I could only smile with half my face, and the result was this weird grimace," says Main, an outgoing person who became self-conscious and reluctant to go out or meet people. "You don't realise how essential a smile is until you can't do it."

Main was lucky: Both times his smile returned within three or four weeks. But about 15 percent of those with Bell's palsy never get their smiles back fully. Others lose their smiles through cancer, stroke or injury. Some, people, such as those with a facial disorder called *Moebius syndrome*, are born without a normal smile.

"My patients have taught me the value of smiling," says Dr. Ralph Manktelow, a plastic surgeon. They say, "Because I can't smile, people think I am unfriendly, sad, angry or depressed, and I can't show them what I am really like." *A smile is a powerful part of our conversation capability*. If you can't smile, you are very limited in your ability to pass on information and relate to other people.

Manktelow and paediatric plastic surgeon, Dr. Ronald Zuker, co-head world renowned Facial Paralysis Team in Toronto Canada, who specialises in the reconstruction of missing or paralysed smiles says, "About 150 patients a year, some 50 of them children, come from around the world with facial paralysis. About 40 of these patients are suitable for the microsurgical procedure, in which surgeons transfer a piece of muscle from the leg to the face. The surgeons attach a nerve to the muscle to make it contract and provide a smile movement. The nerve comes from either the facial nerve on the opposite side of the face or a nerve that normally controls biting. After up to a year of nerve growth, patients develop a smile. If the biting nerve was used, patients first learn to smile by biting."

"With time and practice, most learn to smile without biting, and many smile without even thinking about it," says Manktelow. "The smile is so important, it appears that the brain learns to control the movement of the muscles, and the smile centre takes over to create a spontaneous smile.

After reading the result of the above studies, you will realise how valuable is the gift of natural smile given to you by Nature.

Chapter - 11

May I Wrap it for You the Various Steps to Happiness

And so, with this little wrapping-up chapter, our conversation ends, but not our joint effort and our mutual goal. We walk together, as do all those who have laid strife aside and set their eyes on happiness. This is the other way to pass through the world. It requires no special concepts, no excluding vocabulary, no particular beliefs, only enough hope in the possibility of love and peace to pursue them in one's family, one's job, on the streets, in the stores. Just a little willingness to try to be the kind of person we want to be – one who takes others as they are, who helps when a way to help is clear, who sees innocence in mistakes.

Let us then journey together. The distance to the heart of love is short indeed! Where else could it be but where you are? It is your right to be happy. This is what you were made for. And if you will not resist, happiness will find a way to pour from your heart and fill your days. Simply keep a place within you where it is welcomed, and peace will come and abide with you forever.

Just around the corner

Swami Rama Tirtha said, "If you are not happy as you are, where you are, you will never be happy." Yet everyone is waiting to change one or two things in life to be happy. You suffer from the JATC Syndrome – you believe that happiness is Just Around the Corner! You achieve that one thing and another comes in its place. This goes on all your life.

You can choose to be happy in the worst of circumstances or be miserable with the best. Happiness is a state of mind. When the mind is tranquil, you are happy. However, you are in a constant state of unrest that arises from a feeling of inadequacy. Vedanta helps you change focus to your abundance. When you do that you will be grateful for the bounty. Then the few things you do not have will cease to bother you.

The mind gets turbulent when it is full of unfulfilled desires. You carelessly entertain desires without realising the havoc they cause and the sorrow they breed. All religions warn against the perils of unabashed pursuit of desire. When desire mounts to levels that are no longer sustainable by legal and ethical means people cross the line and enter destructive behaviour.

The Vedanta gives a unique formula for happiness. Happiness is the number of desires fulfilled divided by the desires harboured. You are in the mindless pursuit of fulfilling desires, focussing on the numerator. This will never make you happy. As you fulfill a desire more pop up. The denominator increases, reducing your happiness. Instead shift your attention to the denominator. As you reduce desires, your happiness increases. Eradicate desires and you reach infinite happiness.

The first step to eradicating desire is to ask: Is it in your interest? Is the desire in line with your life's goal? If yes, fulfil the desire. If not, press the delete button.

The next step is to reduce desires by upgrading them. A mother willingly sacrifices her desire for chocolate when her child enjoys it. A student keen on PhD gives up pleasures as well as the safe haven of her home to venture into unknown terrain. When you are inspired with the spiritual goal all desires fade away.

At times, you maybe happy but that happiness is dependent on everything around you being just right. Vedanta promises happiness completely independent of the world. The world is unpredictable, is constantly changing and is a mix of pairs of opposites.

Inner enrichment is inversely proportional to dependence on the world. A spiritually evolved person needs little from the world to be happy but has the capacity to command the resources of the world. He may need only a one-bedroom modest home but has a luxury penthouse apartment. He maybe happy commuting by public transport but has a high end car at his disposal. The surplus he has over his needs puts him in heaven. A less evolved person needs much more from the world. Ironically, he lacks the capability to gain them. There is a huge gap between his needs and his income which makes life hellish.

The Vedanta helps in two ways. It helps leverage your talent, and energies to attain success and prosperity. It also develops you spiritually by which your dependence on the world reduces. You are in bliss!

No more questions, only bliss

If there is one thing equally sought by all, it is happiness. All beings constantly endeavour to seek more happiness through new means of comfort. Science, religion and spirituality all aim at making human beings happier and, therefore, these are not contradictory paths that are at loggerheads with one another. The three paths are complimentary being the essential attributes of the three dimensions of human existence, relating to body, mind and soul.

We have three kinds of bodies – the gross or physical body, the subtle or mental body also known as the psyche and the causal body or soul. When these three bodies combine, a new life is born. The causal body acts as storehouse of all actions, thoughts and desires, and causes the subtle body to combine with the gross body, suitable to bear the fruit of what has been stored. It is like a software programme that is inscribed on the psyche for directing and guiding the physical body accordingly. The combining of the physical body and mental body is called birth and their separation is called *death*.

The characteristic qualities of physical body are movement and growth. Through its faculties of sight, hearing, smell, touch and taste, the physical body gathers impressions of things all around it. All things in the world are transitory in nature, continuously acquiring different forms and states of existence. The human body gathers impressions about them through the five senses. The knowledge that is gathered by the senses falls in the arena of science. Scientific knowledge is thus based on the analysis of information gathered by the senses, which can be subject to scrutiny and verification using physical means. This is why scientists find it difficult to believe in those things, which cannot be proved through experimentation or cannot be perceived through the senses.

Science presents us with various means of comfort for deriving happiness, but true happiness really lies in the mind. A child derives immense pleasure from his toys. As he grows older, he loses interest in them and seeks new means of pleasure. It is not the objects but the state of mind that relates to true happiness. The mind is constantly fed by the senses. It receives impressions stores them and reacts to them. If the mind is not focussed, it does not register impressions.

The characteristic qualities of mind are thinking and knowing. All religions advise us to avoid vices and acquire virtues. The purpose of all religions is to train the mind so as to remain unaffected by the transitory nature of things. Religion teaches us to rise above pride and prejudices and to acquire equanimity so that we can understand and perceive things as they are. A stable mind, which has acquired equanimity, makes one really happy in all circumstances.

Spirituality means to know the real nature of things beyond their transitory nature. It leads to acquiring knowledge of the all-pervading Self and knowing the Self as the source of all happiness and bliss. Then, we come to the end of our quests. Knowledge is in discrimination, in distinguishing between different things or events. With Self-realisation, one attains the highest level of knowledge, of non-duality-that he himself is the source of all bliss. Thus concludes our search for happiness outside.

True happiness lies within

From the moment of birth, every human being craves happiness and not suffering. We look for happiness by fulfilling our emotional needs of love and companionship through our relationships with family, friends and loved ones.

We may derive happiness from them for some time. But the loss of any of our possessions or relations brings untold pain and suffering.

Throughout the ages, the great teachers, sages, saints and philosophers have told us that true happiness does exist. But it does not lie in this world. It can only be found within.

The only permanent source of happiness is God. Some mystics of the east refer to God as *Sat-Chit-Anand*. These words translate respectively as *truth, consciousness and bliss.*

Saints and mystics have been able to realise God within themselves and have shared this knowledge with humanity. They tell us that God is an ocean of light, all love and consciousness.

The soul is a drop of God's essence. Each of us is actually a drop of this blissful awareness. It is only when we identify with our real Self that we become moving drops of bliss on the earth.

The way to tap into this pool is simple. It is only a matter of our attention. We can direct our attention wherever we wish. We can place it on our bodies. We can focus it on our minds. Or, we can concentrate on our souls. This is called *meditation.*

The instruction in how to place our attention on our soul is the domain of spiritual teachers. It we stop paying attention to the eyes and ears for a while and concentrate at the seat of the soul between and behind our eyebrows, we will tap into the source of happiness and bliss awaiting us within.

Happy and you know it?

Who wouldn't like to be happy? And yet, do we really know what leads us to this elusive goal? Are you really happy? Faced with the question, most of us would flounder and prevaricate, for how can you lay claim to absolute happiness? You can say with certainty that you are having fun; you can even say you are joyful and more or less content. But happy or satisfied with life? Well, you could always be happier...

What is happiness? A spot of joy cannot be termed happiness. Nor can a spurt of laughter. Fun at a carnival is just that – a bit of fun, not happiness. Thrill at the sight of a beloved face is not happiness either.

Happiness is much more than these blips. It is more an enduring state of being. A comforting warmth that suffuses your entire being and is there to stay. When you are really happy, a feeling of peace and contentment pervade your being and there's a song in your ear, a spring in your step and a glow in your eyes. A happy person spreads happiness, and the obverse is true as well. Have you noticed how people always welcome those who smile and laugh easily, but how they shy away from depressed souls?

A colleague, who is fond of reading quietly evenings and weekends, is disturbed by her husband's restlessness. He is perpetually moving around, calling up friends and arranging for evening outings. He seems to want to spend as much time as possible away from home and hates to be by himself. His restlessness shows a lack of satisfaction with life and a sharp urge to chase fun and happiness. On the other hand, his wife is a person content with life and quite happy to be by herself.

Happiness is a state of mind that has less to do with changing external circumstances and more to do with your inner self. Research proves beyond doubt that the most developed countries are not necessarily the happiest. In a global happiness survey, the USA came way down 23rd in the list of countries! So acquisition of wealth and possessions don't pave the way to happiness, it seems. The most successful people are not necessarily the ones whose hearts sing the loudest.

Happiness is also subjective and varies from person to person. Would you say Aishwarya Rai Bachchan, beauty queen, successful star, married into Bollywood's most powerful family, is a happy woman? Opinion seems divided. While some would wonder what else could anyone want, others point out the immense pressure she must always be under. And pressure and anxiety are not conducive to a happy state of mind.

Is it possible to engineer happiness for oneself? Surveys have proved that happiness quotient increases as we survey older groups. Some experts say that happiness is embedded in our genes; one survey even proves that happiness depends on geography! Did you know that the Danish are the happiest people in the world? They lead a very balanced life between work and home; most of them leave office by 4.30 pm, use an excellent transport system and send their children to wonderful schools. Danes are very happy with their government, what with 37 hour weeks, 52 weeks of maternity/paternity leave, high unemployment benefits and absolutely safe streets. To top it, Danes take a very realistic view of life and have low expectations.

Ask people casually what makes them really happy and answers range from "a good meal" to "no cribbing" to "big money, big car and big house" to "my children calling out to me" to "movies" to "satisfying sex" to "a good spa treatment." However, well-structured surveys have established that people are happiest when close to their loved ones, when they are in good health and when their expectations aren't very high. This doesn't, however, mean a lack of ambition, but a certain amount of detachment. All of us look for a state of equilibrium, a balanced life and for self-sufficiency.

Most happy people, say experts, consider themselves smarter, healthier and friendlier than others around – they have a high degree of self-esteem. Happy people are also more optimistic and more in control of their lives. The have better relationships with friends and family, better marriages. They seem to realise that deep, caring relationships are an important stepping stone in the pursuit of happiness.

Happy people are also better workers and find challenges at work that they like to meet. On the whole, life for a happy person ends up being a happier experience.

How happy are you?

Find out by taking this life-satisfaction quiz, developed by psychologist Ed Diener, and used to measure happiness worldwide. Indicate your agreement with each item using this 1 to 7 scale. Then add up your total score.

7 Strongly agree; **6** Agree; **5** Slightly agree; **4** Neither agree nor disagree; **3** Slight disagree; **2** Disagree; **1** Strongly disagree

In most ways, my life is close to my deal.   1 2 3 4 5 6 7

The conditions of my life are excellent.
1 2 3 4 5 6 7

I am satisfied with my life
1 2 3 4 5 6 7

So far I have got the important things I want in life
1 2 3 4 5 6 7

If I could live my life over, I would change almost nothing
1 2 3 4 5 6 7

1-35	Extremely satisfied
1-30	Very satisfied
1-25	Slightly satisfied
20	Neutral
15-19	Slightly dissatisfied
10-14	Dissatisfied
5-9	Extremely dissatisfied

Of happiness. When we met, this American college professor looked like a politician with clip-on hair and a polyester tie. We go to breakfast and dinner immediately plunges into the subject that consumes him. "There are tangible benefits to happiness." He says. "Health, creativity, productivity and even altruism are all higher in happy people."

What creativity and work do

Stop right there. Creativity? Aren't all good artists miserable? "You are talking about depressive realism," he says. "That's a school of thought. *It argues that people who see the world clearly are sadder but wiser.* And it is true that happy people tend to be Pollyanna-ish.

"If you ask a group of people, , 'Are you cleverer than others in this room?' Depressed people are more likely to say 'no', and happy people are more likely to say 'yes.' Depressed people tend to be more accurate. But the data show that happy people do better at complex and creative tasks because they are more likely to search for new solutions, while depressed people are more vigilant against making errors."

Diener loves to talk about "the data which show that happy people are more likely to contribute to charity, and their social lives tend to be better. And people in a good mood seem more likely to resist temptation. But if they slip, they can take cheer: They have stronger immune system.

What money does

Happiness even affects our financial lives, since happy people are more of what standard should be used to judge a given society.

Was the best society the one that made its citizens most happy? If so, how can any truly scientific evaluation of happiness be made?

Then Diener started writing. He was so obsessed that he published ten articles in major academic journals in a single year. Economists and gerontologists began asking for help in measuring life satisfaction. And gradually, the world caught up with him.

What social relationships do

On a typical day, the lecture room is packed. Graduate students and faculty members are shoved into corners and sitting cross-legged on the floor. Diener is explaining the results of his latest project, a study of Very Happy People (VHP). The data show that all VHPs have "high-quality social relationships," but that just raises another question: Do high-quality relationships make VHPs very happy, or are you born with a "set point" for happiness that keeps you at a certain mood level no matter what you do? "Some people claim that temperament is everything to happiness," he says. "So there is no point in really improving society in terms of happiness because we're all on a *hedonic treadmill.* Your mother dies and it makes you unhappy, but a few days later, you're back to where you were before."

Then there is the widowhood data: Three years before their husbands die, as their spouses get sick, the wives' life satisfaction starts dropping. Five years after hubby's demise, the widows are almost back to normal.

What the "right ingredients" do

Diener opens the floor to questions, and the first one comes from a professor with a new baby. All these data are fine, but she needs some straight answers quick. "How can I make my kid happy?" she asks.

Diener shakes his head. He's heard this one before. "There is no key to happiness. It's more like baking a cake. You have to have a lot of flour and___"

"Eggs!" the students shout. "Sugar!" "___and you have got to have them in the right mix," he continues.

"So what are the right ingredients?" A mom asks.

Everyone laughs, knowing that his real answer is that any talk-show host can give advice, but Ed Diener has a great and steadfast goal: to bring the rigours of science to our aspirations, to lay schematics over the mysteries of the heart, to become the Darwin of human happiness.

"Certainly one of those ingredients is social relationship," he begins. "Another is temperament. And having long-term goals that are congruent with one another, and that are pleasurable to work for. If you want to be a lawyer but you hate conflict, you're going to be messed up."

And beyond that? We're just going to have to wait on the data.

How to pursue happiness?

Every day, it seems, the media floods us with superficial, simplistic "pop-psych" advice about happiness. The relentless message is that there's something we're supposed to do to be happy – make the right choices, or have the right set of beliefs about ourselves.

Coupled with this is the notion that happiness is a permanent condition. If we're not joyful all the time, we conclude there's a problem.

Yet what most people experience is not a permanent state of happiness. It is something more ordinary, a mixture of what essayist Huge Prather once called, "unsolved problems, ambiguous victories and vague defeats – with few moments of clear peace."

Maybe, you wouldn't say yesterday was a happy day, because you had a misunderstanding with your boss. But weren't there moments of happiness, moments of clear peace? Now that you think about it, wasn't there a letter from an old friend, or a stranger who asked where you got such a great haircut? You remember having a bad day, yet those good moments occurred.

Happiness is like a visitor, a genial, exotic aunt who turns up when you least expect her, orders an extravagant round of drinks and then disappears, trailing a lingering scent of gardenias. You cannot command her appearance; you can only appreciate her when she does show up. And you cannot force happiness to happen – but you can make sure you are aware of it when it does.

While you're walking home with a head full of problems, try to notice the sun set on the windows of the city on fire. Listen to the shouts of kids playing in the fading light, and feel your spirits rise, just from having paid attention.

Happiness is an attitude, not a condition. It is cleaning the Venetian blinds while listening to your favourite singer, or spending a pleasant hour organising your cupboard. Happiness is your family assembled at dinner. It is in the present, not in the distant promise of a "someday when..." How much luckier we are – and how much more happiness we experience – if we can fall in love with the life we're living.

Happiness is choice. Reach out for it at the moment it appears, like a balloon drifting seawards in a bright blue sky.

Part – III
THOUGHTS TO HAPPINESS

Food for Thought

1. Life would be infinitely happier if we could only be born at the age of 80 and gradually approach to 18 – **American author and humourist Mark Twain**
2. Happiness is not something readymade. It comes from your own action – **The XIV Dalai Lama**
3. You will never be happy if you continue to search for what happiness consist of. You will never live if you are looking for the meaning of life – **Albert Camus**
4. Caring about others, running the risk of feeling, and leaving an impact on people, bring happiness – **Harold Kushner**
5. Attachment is the great fabricator of illusions; reality can be attained only by someone who is detached – **Simon Weil**
6. Sometimes your joy is the source of your smile, but sometimes your smile can be the source of your joy – **Thich Nhat Hanh**
7. Forget not that the earth delights to feel your bare feet and the winds long to play with your hair – **Kahlil Gibran**
8. Living on earth is expensive, but it does include a free trip around the sun every year – **Anonymous**
9. Every breath we take, every move we make, can be filled with peace and joy...we need only to be awake and alive in the present moment - **Thich Nhat Hanh**
10. For myself I am an optimist, it does not seem to be much use being anything else – **Winston Churchill**
11. Those who are free of resentful thoughts surely find peace – **Gautam Buddha**
12. Nothing thicker than a knife's blade separates happiness from melancholy – **Virginia Woolf**
13. Tension is who you think you should be. Relaxations is who you are – **Chinese Proverb**
14. A hearty laugh gives one a dry cleaning, while a good cry is a wet wash - **Puzant K. Thomajan**
15. I once wanted to become an atheist but I gave up...I was told they have no holidays – **Henny Youngman**

16. Nothing can dim the light which shines from within - **Mayo Angelou**
17. Some people, no matter how old they get, never lose their beauty – they merely move it from their faces into their heart – **American photographer, artist and humorist Martin Buxbaun**
18. Common sense and a sense of humour are the same thing, moving at different speeds. A sense of humour is just common sense, dancing – **American philosopher William James**
19. I keep telling people, smile, you will look young; it is an exercise! If you don't smile, your face will look dull – **Asha Bhosle**
20. Laughter is the sun that drives winter from the human face – **Victor Hugo, Playwright and Visual Artist**
21. I have failed over and over again in my life. And that's why I succeed – **Michael Jordan**
22. All that we know is nothing, we are merely crammed waste paper baskets, unless we are in touch with that which laughs at all our knowing – **David Herbert Lawrence**
23. Exercise is king; nutrition is queen. Put them together and you have got a kingdom - **Jack Lalanne**
24. As we cultivate peace and happiness in ourselves, we also nourish peace and happiness in those we love – **Thich Nhat Hanh**
25. The secret of happiness is freedom, and the secret of freedom is courage – **Thucydides**
26. The love deeply in one direction makes us more loving in all others – **Swetchine**
27. A man is not old until regrets take the place of dreams – **American actor John Barrymore**
28. Change your thoughts and you change your world – **Norman Vincent Peale**
29. We are all born for love. It is the principle of existence, and its only end – **Oprah Winfrey**
30. Positive anything is better than negative nothing – **Elbert Hubbard**
31. A contented mind is the greatest blessing a man can enjoy in this world – **Joseph Addison**
32. Always remember to be happy because you never know who's falling in love with your smile – **Anonymous**

33. At the height of laughter, the universe is flung into a kaleidoscope of new possibilities – **Jean Houston**

34. You grow up the day, you have your first real laugh – at yourself – **Ethel Barrymore**

35. Eventually you will come to understand that love heals everything, and love is all there is – **Gary Zukav**

36. We all live with the objective of being happy; our lives are all different and yet the same – **Norman Vincent Peale**

37. Action may not always bring happiness; but there is no happiness without action – **Benjamin Disraell**

38. Dare to Dream, Life is a challenge, Meet it!, Life is a dream, Realise it!, Life is a game, Play it!, Life is love, Enjoy it! – **Sathya Sai Baba**

39. We tend to forget that happiness doesn't come as a result of getting something we don't have, but rather of recognising and appreciating what we do have – **Frederick Keonig**

40. Live For Today, Yesterday is but a dream; tomorrow is only a vision. But today well-lived, makes every yesterday a dream of happiness and every tomorrow a vision of hope – **Kalidasa**

41. My own understanding is that there is nothing more valuable than laughter. Laughter brings you closest to prayer. In fact only laughter is left in you when you are total. In everything else, you remain partial, even in lovemaking, you remain partial. But when you have a really heartfelt belly laugh, all the parts of your being – the physiological, the psychological, the spiritual – they all vibrate in one single tune, they all vibrate in harmony. Hence, laughter relaxes. And relaxation is spiritual. Laughter brings you to earth, brings you down from your stupid ideas of being holier-than-thou. Laughter brings you to reality as it is. The world is a play of God, a cosmic joke. And unless you understand it as a cosmic joke, you will never be able to understand the ultimate mystery. I am all for jokes, I am all for laughter – **Osho**

42. Happiness is having a large, caring, close-knit family in another city – **George Burns**

43. It is the test of a good religion whether you can joke about it – **Gilbert K Chesterton**

44. It's better to laugh about things that can't be changed – **Anna Jokai, writer**

45. Raising kids is part joy and part guerrilla warfare – **Ed Asner, actor**

46. The day the Lord created hope was probably the same day, he created spring – **Bern Williams**
47. Not a shred of evidence exists in favour of the idea that life is serious – **Brendan Gill**
48. Nothing shows a man's character more than what he laughs at – **Geothe**
49. Choose a job you love, and you will never have to work a day in your life – **Confucius**
50. Compassion automatically brings happiness and calmness. Then, even if you receive disturbing news, it will be easier to take, as your mind is still – **Dalai Lama**
51. Un-forgiveness is the poison you drink everyday, hoping that the other person will die - **Debble Ford**
52. If we could see the miracle of a single flower clearly, our whole life would change – **Buddha**
53. Happy Always – Happiness is when what you think, what you say, and what you do are in harmony – **M.K. Gandhi**
54. This is my "depressed stance". When you're depressed. It makes a lot of difference how you stand. The worst thing you can do is straighten up and hold your head high because then you'll start to feel better. If you're going to get any joy out of being depressed, you've got to stand like this – **Charlie Brown**
55. If you want to be happy, be – **Leo Tolstoy**
56. If you see ten troubles coming down the road, you can be sure that nine will run into the ditch before they reach you – **Calvin Coolidge**
57. You can't get enough of what you don't need to make you happy – **Eric Hoffer**
58. An optimist is the human personification of spring – **Susan J Bissonette**
59. A good laugh and a long sleep are the best cures in the doctor's book – **Irish Proverb**
60. There is no such thing as pursuit of happiness, there is only the discovery of joy – **Joyce Grenfell**
61. Why is it that when your cup of happiness is full, somebody always jogs your elbow? - **Helen Rowland**

62. Facing Crises – Man is bound by his own action except when it is performed for the sake of sacrifice. Therefore, do efficiently perform your duty, free from attachment, for the sake of sacrifice alone. In this world that real soul has no use whatsoever for things done nor for things not done; nor has he selfish dependence of any kind on any creature. Therefore, go on efficiently doing your duty without attachment... **Bhagavad Gita 3.9, 18-19**

63. Pursuit of Happiness – People say : "There is so much suffering in the world; how can you be happy?" By becoming unhappy, you only add to unhappiness, isn't it? You can be happy now, right now – wherever you are. And you can still do all that you want to do. We have a wrong notion that only when we have ambition and desire we will be able to make progress. It is not so. You can make better progress without this ambition, without this feverishness. To be happy just needs a little skill. Be happy! This is an order as well as a blessing - **Sri Sri Ravi Shankar**

64. The greatest happiness of the greatest number is the foundation of morals - **Jeremy Bentham**

65. Happiness is a mystery, like religion, and should never be rationalised - **G.K. Chesterton**

66. The small share of happiness attainable by man exist only in so far as he is able to cease to think of himself – **Theodor Reik**

67. All questions at the public meeting that day were about life beyond the grave. The Master only laughed and did not give a single answer. To his disciples, who demanded to know the reason for his evasiveness, he later said, "Have you observed that it is precisely those who do not know what to do with this life who want another that will last forever?" "But is there life after death or is there not?" persisted a disciple. "Is there life before death?" said the Master enigmatically – **Anthony de Mello**

68. What makes a river so restful to people is that it doesn't have any doubt – it is sure to get where it is going, and it doesn't want to go anywhere else – **Hal Boyle**

69. The Present Moment – The secret of health for both mind and body is not to mourn for the past, nor to worry about the future, but to live the present moment wisely and earnestly – **Gautama Buddha**

70. Life is either a daring adventure or nothing – **Helen Keller**
71. God is the experience of looking at a tree and saying 'Ah...!' – **Khalil Gibran**
72. Immature love says : "I love you because I need you." Mature love says : "I need you because I love you." – **Mahatma Gandhi**
73. Love doesn't make the world go round. Love is what makes the ride worthwhile - **Franklin P. Jones**
74. Minds are like parachutes: They only function when open – **Thomas R. Dewar**
75. **Did you know?**

(i) In Indiana, USA there was once a law preventing people from travelling on buses within four hours of eating garlic.

(ii) The word, 'bride' comes from an ancient German word meaning 'one who cooks.'

(iii) In 1857, Queen Victoria's rat-catcher was paid more than the poet Laureate, Lord Tennyson.

(iv) When ill, Emperor Meneuk-II of Ethiopia would eat pages from the Bible.

SELF IMPROVEMENT/PERSONALITY DEVELOPMENT

    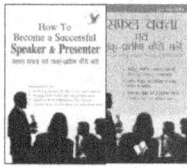 

All books available at www.vspublishers.com

HINDI LITERATURE

TALES & STORIES

MUSIC (संगीत)

All Books Fully Coloured

MAGIC & FACT (जादू एवं तथ्य)

MYSTERIES (रहस्य)

ACADEMIC BOOKS

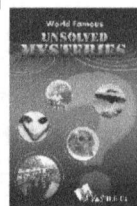   

All books available at www.vspublishers.com

www.ingramcontent.com/pod-product-compliance
Lightning Source LLC
Chambersburg PA
CBHW070336230426
43663CB00011B/2345